Isle of Wight

Jackie & Chris Par

Jackie Parry

With a degree in French and German, Ja.
experience in tourism and is a Blue Badge Guide, ...
foreign visitors around Southern England, in particular the Isle o. ...
Born and raised in Portsmouth, she has travelled and worked extensively
both abroad and in the United Kingdom. She lives once again in her
home city with her husband and son.

Chris Parry

Chris Parry is a naval officer who combines a busy, highly stimulating
career with a keen interest in history and outdoor pursuits.

Preface

The authors have received neither request nor payment for the inclusion
of any of the amenities or businesses named or recommended in this
guide.
It has been our intention to present an objective, balanced view of what
is available on the Isle of Wight for the benefit of all visitors.

Dedication

For Jonathan

Acknowledgements

Thanks are due to:

The Staff of Yarmouth Tourist Office, in particular Diana Holbrook
and Maureen Finn, for a warm welcome, cheerfulness and excellent
knowledge of their Island. Sophie Jeffery and Sue Emerson
of Isle of Wight Tourism. Linda Smith.

Landmark Visitors Guide

Isle of Wight

Jackie & Chris Parry

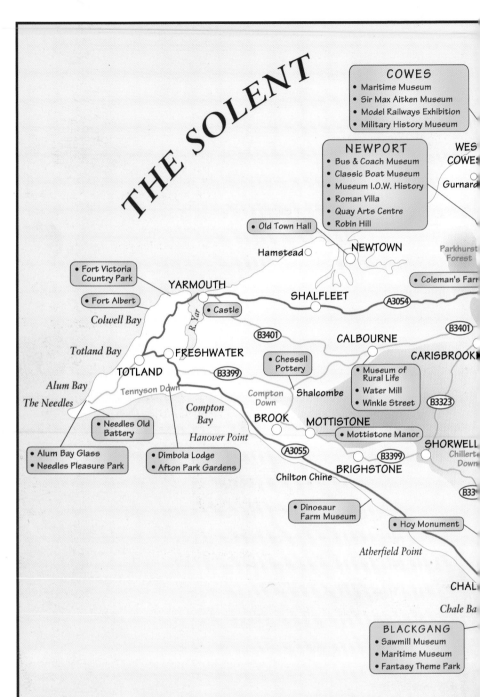

THE SOLENT

COWES
- Maritime Museum
- Sir Max Aitken Museum
- Model Railways Exhibition
- Military History Museum

NEWPORT
- Bus & Coach Museum
- Classic Boat Museum
- Museum I.O.W. History
- Roman Villa
- Quay Arts Centre
- Robin Hill

WES COWE:

Gurnard

- Old Town Hall

Hamstead○   **NEWTOWN**   Parkhurst Forest

- Coleman's Farr

- Fort Victoria Country Park

YARMOUTH   **SHALFLEET**   A3054

- Fort Albert

Colwell Bay   R. Yar   • Castle

Totland Bay   B3401   **CALBOURNE**   B3401

FRESHWATER   **CARISBROOK**

TOTLAND   B3399   • Museum of Rural Life

Alum Bay   *Tennyson Down*   *Compton Down*   Shalcombe   • Water Mill

The Needles   *Compton Bay*   • Winkle Street   B3323

BROOK   **MOTTISTONE**

- Needles Old Battery   *Hanover Point*   • Mottistone Manor   **SHORWELL**
Chillerto Down

- Alum Bay Glass
- Needles Pleasure Park   • Dimbola Lodge
- Afton Park Gardens   A3055   **BRIGHSTONE**   B3399   B33

Chilton Chine

- Dinosaur Farm Museum

- Hoy Monument

Atherfield Point

CHAL

Chale Ba

BLACKGANG
- Sawmill Museum
- Maritime Museum
- Fantasy Theme Park

ISLE OF WIGHT

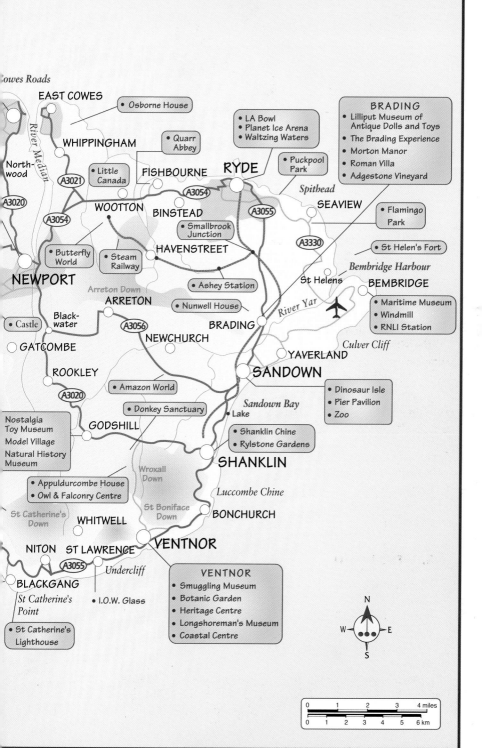

Cowes Roads

EAST COWES
• Osborne House

WHIPPINGHAM

River Medina

Northwood

FISHBOURNE

• Quarr Abbey

• LA Bowl
• Planet Ice Arena
• Waltzing Waters

RYDE

• Puckpool Park

Spithead

BRADING
• Lilliput Museum of Antique Dolls and Toys
• The Brading Experience
• Morton Manor
• Roman Villa
• Adgestone Vineyard

A3021

• Little Canada

A3054

A3055

SEAVIEW

A3020

A3054

WOOTTON

BINSTEAD

• Smallbrook Junction

HAVENSTREET

A3330

• Flamingo Park

• St Helen's Fort

Bembridge Harbour

• Butterfly World

• Steam Railway

St Helens

BEMBRIDGE

NEWPORT

Arreton Down

ARRETON

• Ashey Station

• Nunwell House

River Yar

• Maritime Museum
• Windmill
• RNLI Station

Blackwater

• Castle

A3056

NEWCHURCH

BRADING

Culver Cliff

GATCOMBE

YAVERLAND

ROOKLEY

• Amazon World

SANDOWN

A3020

• Donkey Sanctuary

Sandown Bay

• Dinosaur Isle
• Pier Pavilion
• Zoo

Nostalgia Toy Museum
Model Village
Natural History Museum

GODSHILL

• Lake

• Shanklin Chine
• Rylstone Gardens

• Appuldurcombe House
• Owl & Falconry Centre

Wroxall Down

SHANKLIN

St Catherine's Down

WHITWELL

St Boniface Down

Luccombe Chine

BONCHURCH

NITON   ST LAWRENCE

VENTNOR

A3055

Undercliff

BLACKGANG

• I.O.W. Glass

VENTNOR
• Smuggling Museum
• Botanic Garden
• Heritage Centre
• Longshoreman's Museum
• Coastal Centre

St Catherine's Point

• St Catherine's Lighthouse

N
W — E
S

0   1   2   3   4 miles
0   1   2   3   4   5   6 km

Contents

TOP TWELVE TIPS

St Catherine's Point
Lighthouse

Here is a personal choice of twelve
favourite attractions that should give
most visitors a broad appreciation of
what the Isle of Wight has to offer.

- Osborne House – Victoria's Retreat
- Carisbrooke Castle – bite-size history
- Isle of Wight Steam Railway – nostalgia rules
- Amazon World – sub-tropical surprise
- Tennyson Trail – great views and worth the effort
- Ventnor Botanic Gardens – visually impressive
- St Catherine's Point Lighthouse – southernmost sentinel
- Brading Roman Villa – mosaics and more
- Dimbola Lodge – cameras, cakes and coffee
- Quarr Abbey – quiet, but evocative
- Dinosaur Isle – hands-on bones experience
- Newtown Estuary – coastal Nature Reserve

KEY FOR SYMBOLS

Wightbytes

Child logo – with an age at the top of the
symbol indicating 12 (under 12) or 7 (under 7).
The number at the bottom of the symbol is
a tolerance threshold assessed in minutes.

There is also an umbrella symbol
indicating rainy day potential.

Introduction

Oh! what a snug little island!
A right little, tight, little Island!
Thomas Dibdin 1771-1842

Why should anyone want to go to the Isle of Wight? In the first place, travelling to any island by sea has a hint of excitement and the exotic about it; the crossing not only places the traveller in a normally unfamiliar sea environment, but also induces a definite break in thinking and routine. The passage to the Isle of Wight has all the thrill of going abroad, but without the loss of those familiar features which make the United Kingdom home.

of the south-east of England. It has a reasonably balanced diversity of town and country landscapes, of brashness and sophistication, of modernity and tradition, enabling it to cope with a broad spectrum of tastes. It has a varied, stimulating historical and literary heritage, with enough monuments, curiosities and memorials to satisfy the most enthusiastic professional tourist or the most incurable romantic.

Furthermore, it is suitable for both long and short trips and the Island's diverse, yet self-contained and seemingly unchanging, appeal often induces visitors to return. Finally, there is the mild climate and sea air, which has been known, particularly since early Victorian times, for its restorative and inspirational powers.

Whatever the attraction or reason, visitors have always come in their thousands and continue to do so, despite the magnetic pull of holidays abroad. J B Priestley probably summed it up best when he said that one, 'might take one glance at the Island as something on a map, and then decide to give it a couple of hours. But you can spend days and days exploring the Isle of Wight, which, if you are really interested, begins magically enlarging itself for you.'

Some people have travelled to the Island in the past as eccentrics, recluses or fugitives or in search of inspiration. A great many come because of an intuitive need to return to a place in which they remember spending happy childhood holidays. Many of these also retire to the Island while others seek a commercial opportunity.

Both scenically and culturally, the Isle of Wight is a miniature replica

CLIMATE

The climate of the Isle of Wight is affected mainly by the prevalence of sea breezes and by the high incidence of south-westerly winds. Topography also plays a part, which is why the coast between Blackgang and

Luccombe including Ventnor, is so mild, with its protection from all but southerly winds and its exposure to the sunny south. Conversely, Ventnor in summer is slightly cooler owing to its cliff-top position in relative shade at the start and end of the day and the cool south-westerlies which prevail at that time of year. Overall, however, throughout the year, the Island is between one and two degrees higher in temperature than the mainland.

WHEN TO GO

There is something to do on the Island all the year round, despite the seasonal emphasis of some businesses and attractions. The variety of attractions in a small area and the transport infrastructure mean that the vagaries of the weather can be mitigated at any time. However, opening times of most attractions are curtailed in the winter months and some, more obviously 'tourist-orientated', close down altogether. The larger, less seasonally dependent attractions and those in the towns generally stay open during winter daylight hours. It is always worth checking by telephone or with Isle of Wight Tourism before planning a visit out of season.

The two periods from Easter to early summer and September through to the end of October offer the best balance of weather and amenities, when the popular resorts and attractions are not too crowded. From June through to August anyone wanting sun and a beach-centred holiday is likely to be most content. These periods are the most suitable for longer trips of one or two weeks. In winter months, the weekend break or day trip is likely to prove the most rewarding, although themed trips, based on particular interests may extend a visit. Needless to say, accommodation is normally cheaper outside the season, but choice will be somewhat more restricted.

Ventnor

Those with special interests, such as bird-watching, will wish to gear their visits to periods of optimum activity. Migrant birds are best observed on one of the main migration routes in spring or autumn. Walkers and cyclists will find suitable routes all the year round. Sailing and other water sports are naturally inhibited in winter, although the more experienced, adventurous wind and board surfers and yachties will no doubt find the challenge exhilarating.

GEOGRAPHY

The Isle of Wight is a lozenge shaped island, measuring 23 miles (37km) from the Needles in the west to Bembridge Foreland in the east and 13 miles (21km) from Cowes in the north to St Catherine's Point in the south. It is about 60 miles (97km) all round and covers about 155 sq miles (401km^2), which hold a population of 127,000. It fits snugly against the opposite mainland of Hampshire and is separated by the narrow stretch of water known as the Solent, which varies in width from 6 miles (9.7km) to about three-quarters of a mile (1km).

A spine of chalk hills, or downs, running east to west, from Sandown to the Needles, virtually bisects the Island and another outcrop behind St Catherine's and Shanklin hems in the Undercliff, on the south-east side of the lozenge. The main river is the Medina, which almost traverses the Island from south to north, passing through Newport and emptying into the sea at Cowes. Numerous bays, chines and tidal creeks indent the coast.

Double tide

Wightbyte

An odd Solent phenomenon is its double high tide, which was so distinct as to be mentioned in Bede's 'History of the English Church and People' in the eighth century. The first tide comes straight up the English Channel through the Needles Channel from the west and produces the first high water. Two hours later, another tide, which started out in the Atlantic about twelve hours before the first one, and flogged its way around the top of Scotland and through the Dover Straight, arrives from the east. Just as the (first) tide is starting to ebb, it returns to a high tide again (with the second), before ebbing rapidly to complete the cycle. This has given the Solent distinctive tidal features and considerable problems for the unwary, careless navigator or sporting sailor.

GEOLOGY

Geologically, the Island presents a unique and complex amalgam of layers or strata. Specialist geologists enthuse about the concentration of so many different types of rock and geological periods in one small area, but even the casual but perceptive visitor will note the sudden changes in topography and rock types across the Island. The very old Wealden

Continued on page 14...

Above: Boat trip from Yarmouth Pierhead
Below: Start of the Round the World Race at Cowes

Opposite page; Top: Tourist Office at Yarmouth
Bottom: Crazy Golf in Shanklin

Beds near Sandown and the compelling east-west spine of chalk are supplemented elsewhere by clays, gravels and greensands.

Whitecliff Bay is a striking example of where the chalk and clay meet, to be joined by a whole sequence of important sedimentary layers in order of the time they were deposited. Consequently, the Island is well-known for its fossil finds: the Wealden Beds have revealed the fossilised skeletons of large reptiles and the whole coastline of West Wight from Atherstone Ledge through Alum Bay to Hamstead has produced prolific numbers of plant and animal fossils.

Underlying 'Blue Slipper' clay was responsible for the landslip (hence its name) that caused the Undercliff in the south-east of the Island. All in all, it is a geologist's paradise and those who want to delve more deeply should visit Dinosaur Isle in Sandown. It opened in April 2001 close to Sandown Zoo and now houses the Museum of Isle of Wight Geology.

The Isle of Wight's existence as an Island dates from about 8,000 years ago, when the sea breached the continuous chalk ridge between the Needles and the Isle of Purbeck, in mainland Dorset. Before that event, a river had flowed down Southampton Water and emptied into the sea via the channel of the eastern Solent somewhere south of Littlehampton.

BRIEF HISTORY

Archaeological remains have revealed human settlement from the Old Stone Age and implements from at least Palaeolithic times (half a million years to 12,000 years ago).

Further evidence of settlement is provided by Neolithic (2300-1900 BC) long barrows along the Downs and numerous Bronze Age (about 1,900 BC onwards) round barrows. Iron Age occupation (from about 550 BC), demonstrated by ancient field systems and one hill fort on Chillerton Down, gave way to Roman domination after Claudius' invasion of Britain in 43 AD.

The Island, called *Ynys yr wyth* (the Island of the channel), was captured by the II Legion, commanded by the future emperor Vespasian. To the Romans, the Island was known as 'Vectis' and its agricultural output is attested by the surviving remains of several large villas, including those that can be seen at Brading and Newport. A possible fort underlies the fortifications at Carisbrooke, but no Roman town or road has been identified.

In the confused settlement after the Roman era in the fifth century, the Island was initially seized and held by Jutish war-bands, but they, in turn, were replaced by West Saxons. According to Bede, the inhabitants of the Island had remained defiantly pagan up to that point, but from then on had their own bishop, subject to the See of Winchester.

The rest of the Anglo-Saxon period was punctuated with raids by Scandinavian or Viking marauders. One most memorably led to a sea battle at Brading won by Alfred the Great's forces in 896. After the Norman Conquest in 1066, the Island was granted to William I's close friend and senior military commander, William fitzOsbern. He started the building of Carisbrooke castle with a motte-and-bailey structure and endowed its priory and six Island churches. In 1100, the lordship of the Island passed to the de Redvers family who held it until 1293, when Edward I purchased the lordship and took it into Crown hands.

During the late medieval and Tudor period, the Island became progressively more involved and integrated with events and personalities on the mainland. From the fourteenth to the sixteenth century, the Isle of Wight and the coastline opposite were constantly exposed to raids by the French, especially during the 100 Years' War and in the reign of Henry VIII (1509-47). In the Civil Wars of 1642-8, the Island assumed national prominence when Charles I was held at Carisbrooke and tried to escape while negotiating terms with Parliament and the Army.

The Island's subsequent history was shaped by the importance of the Solent as a focus for expanding international trade and its association with the rise of the Royal Navy. During the long periods of war in the eighteenth century, the Isle of Wight was notorious for widespread smuggling and excise evasion, while it helped meet the needs of the growing military and commercial effort. Thereafter, the patronage of Queen Victoria at Osborne and the rise of tourism did much to transform the Island into an attractive and popular resort.

Today, despite continuing agricultural activity, the Island relies heavily on visitors, leisure activities and residential development to sustain its vitality and economy. Improved transport links with the mainland allow people to settle on the Island and commute to work across the water. Although the Isle of Wight shares some services with nearby Hampshire, since 1974 it has been a separate administrative county. It is geographically the largest parliamentary constituency in the country.

FLORA AND FAUNA

This modest introduction is not intended for the specialist, but for those who may feel that a trip to the Isle of Wight presents an ideal opportunity to introduce themselves or their children to the pleasures of the Island's wildlife. The mild climate and sea air, separation from the mainland and the different habitats induced by the topography and geology are reflected in its wildlife. Many species found on the mainland opposite, such as the grey squirrel, the nuthatch and the sand lizard, are not found in the Island.

Mammals

There are thirty-seven species of mammal on the Island. Hedgehogs and moles are common and there are ten species of bat, while rabbits and hares are evenly distributed throughout. Badgers, foxes, weasels and stoats are frequently seen in country areas, together with the occasional otter, which has swum from the mainland, but rarely stays. The only deer have been introduced on farms as stock.

The Isle of Wight is one of the few places where the red squirrel can be seen and is thriving. They are plentiful in the Island's woodlands, particularly in Parkhurst Forest. A naturalist recently stated with some irony, 'The grey squirrel occasionally comes over on the ferries, but has not become established here'.

Birds

The Island supports a changing resident and migratory bird population. There are a great many sea and coastal nesting locations, with the main sites at Freshwater and Culver Cliff. Cormorants, shags, wintering grebes, waders, wildfowl (Canada geese) can all be found in northern creeks and around Brading (RSPB Bird Hide). A recent decline in guillemots and razorbills has been accompanied by a rise in peregrines, which have colonised Freshwater, and fulmars, which can be seen from Blackgang to Culver Cliff.

The barn owl is a common sight at dusk, although the tawny owl is not seen on the Island. Other distinctive species are: the green and great spotted woodpeckers, the collared dove and a few pairs of Dartford warblers. Ravens and rooks, which have recently been under threat, have managed to survive modern changes in their habitats.

For migratory birds, the best time of year is from March to May at St Catherine's Lighthouse where the passage is from east to west and where special perches have been set up. Divers, waders, auks, terns and skuas can be seen, as well as ducks and large numbers of smaller land birds. In autumn, Fort Victoria on the Freshwater Peninsula is the best vantage point for witnessing the reverse migration from east to west.

Reptiles

These include the grass snake, the adder, slow-worm and common lizard while frogs, toads and three types of newt are widely distributed.

Butterflies

The Island is particularly rich in butterflies. The grass of the downland, which has its own distinctive species of plants, is home to a wide variety, including the chalk hill blue and the adonis blue. The small blue can be found in relative abundance around Compton and Afton Downs. Wight is a good habitat for fritillaries; the dark green and silver-washed are found on the Downs, Parkhurst Forest holds small and brown pearl-bordered and marsh varieties, Newtown and Hamstead the high brown. The Glanville fritillary is unique (in the UK) to the Isle of Wight and is found from late spring along the cliffs in the south-east of the Island.

Wild flowers

Two woodland flowers, which thrive on the Island, are, uniquely, the wood calamint and the more widely known wild columbine. Most woodland supports wild garlic with its distinctive aroma and non-native cord-grass has colonised the edges and mudflats of most of the northern estuaries and creeks. There are also twenty-seven species of orchid. Some of them are plentiful, such as the common spotted or the early-purple; others are less common, but can be found on the chalk downs, such as the bee and the pyramidal orchids.

In addition to the miles of largely unspoilt countryside, there are many dedicated woodland and wildlife trails and walks, which have been set up by the Forest Enterprise and other agencies. Some of these are mentioned in the text, but for a full list, visitors should obtain the details available from Isle of Wight Tourism. The Isle of Wight Council's Countryside Section (☎ (01983) 823893) also organises and publishes an excellent programme of countryside events from April to September, mostly based around walks. There is

Above: Red Squirrel

Left: Locally grown grapes

Below: One of many coastal cliff paths

no need to book in most cases, but there may be a nominal charge.

NATURE AREAS

A particular favourite is **Walter's Copse** and **Town Copse** (National Trust) at Newtown, with their well-established and accessible path systems. Newtown is a delightful silted creek, which has salt marshes, tidal mud flats and shingle banks. There are black-headed gulls in profusion, together with wild fowl, waders and terns. Cord-grass grows in abundance and it is just about the only place on the Island to hear and see the nightingale, which thrives on the blackthorn and damp thickets.

Other places suitable for laymen, with car parks or lay-bys, to explore the wildlife are:

- **America Wood**, Shanklin (Woodland Trust).

- **Borthwood Copse**, Alverstone (National Trust).

- **Brighstone Forest**, mixed woodland walk over about 2.5 miles (4km).

- **Combley Great Wood**, near Havenstreet.

- **Firestone Copse**, near Wootton (Forest Enterprise) has way-marked walks.

- **Parkhurst Forest** (Forest Enterprise), 2.5-mile (4km) walk with shorter trails.

- **River Medina**, Newport has 300 acres (122 hectares) of salt-marsh, woodland and river, with a 2-mile (3.2km) walk, starting at Newport Quay.

CHARACTER

Conscious of its pre-Victorian remoteness and its tradition of sturdy self-reliance, the Island is proud of its separation – rather than isolation – from the rest of the United Kingdom. Its people have stoutly resisted all attempts to link it with the mainland by means of a bridge or tunnel. 'Caulkheads', those born on the Island and from established Island families, are still keen to maintain their status against the 'overners', who are not natives by birth and 'grockles', as tourists are known. Denizens of Ryde or Yarmouth still talk about 'going to England' or, wryly, refer to England as the North Island.

Agriculture and market gardening (particularly organic) enterprises are thriving although employing fewer people every year. The Island's industry and manufacturing base is excessively light for a local mixed economy and the Island depends overwhelmingly on attracting visitors.

In a time of unprecedented social and economic change, the Island is having to confront the dilemma of attracting more visitors to sustain its economy while maintaining an equitable life-style for its inhabitants, most of whom settled on the Island to get away from the accelerated pace of modern life. This is partly achieved by concentrating much of the more commercial elements and development in a few coastal areas and getting on with life regardless. However, a constant tension exists between forces tending to turn the Island into a massive theme park and those seeking to preserve its unique character and community.

Even today, its diversity is its salvation, despite the fact that the

Family on the beach

Island subsists so much on tourism, and it is a mistake to see the Island community as a single entity. There are considerable differences between the character of the coastal towns and that of the rural areas, between long established families and newcomers, even between Ryde and Cowes. A glance at the *Isle of Wight County Press* will show that thriving, vibrant communities, (some of the parish churches are evidence of this) rub shoulders with less favoured areas.

For all that, the 'native' Islanders are a hardy, resilient bunch, used to surviving crises and economic fluctuations. The Garden Isle scarcely needs to sell itself in its present form and visitors are always afforded a warm welcome. There are constraints on growth if the Island is to maintain its fragile balance of commercialism, rural charm, unspoilt landscapes and community. A holiday or stay in the Island represents excellent value for money if the visitor enjoys the diversity of the Island's attractions, the most striking of which are free, and perhaps limits the intensity of his or her, but more especially the children's, participation in the more blatantly commercial aspects.

Finally, this guide has been arranged to take into account three main geographical areas on the Isle of Wight, which correspond to the ports of entry from the mainland. Therefore, we start with the eastern part of the Island, most readily accessible from Portsmouth through Fishbourne and Ryde, then the central part (accessed from Southampton through Cowes) and finally the west and Back of Wight, based on Yarmouth and the crossing from Lymington.

1. East Wight

The eastern part of the Island attracts most visitors because of its established coastal resorts, its communication network and, within its own terms, its extensive tourist infrastructure. As well as Ryde, the front-line seaside towns are Sandown, Shanklin and Ventnor, which, together with Brading and other satellites, offer attractions that appeal to a range of tastes and enthusiasms. It does get busy in the summer but there are enough places to escape to, particularly in the hinterland, when the crowds get too much or the weather disappoints. A foot passenger arriving through Ryde or Fishbourne can easily move around eastern Wight and in season will find that he hardly needs a car to enjoy the rest of the Island as well.

FISHBOURNE TO RYDE

Fishbourne Creek is dominated by the main Wightlink car ferry terminal. Home to the Royal Victoria Yacht Club it is much frequented by yachtsmen. A short walk from Fishbourne and visible from the ferry are the distinctive towers of Quarr Abbey, built between 1908 and 1912. The spectacular red-brick Benedictine house, designed by Dom Paul Bellot, a pioneer of twentieth-century Expressionism, was built as a permanent home for a community of displaced French monks from Solesmes, near Le Mans; today they number about twenty. The abbey church, in particular, is famous for its high pointed arches and windows.

Wightbyte

Quarr

Quarr derives its name from the nearby limestone quarries, originally worked by the Romans. The stone was used for the building of the old abbey, as well as the Norman cathedrals at Winchester and Chichester.

The abbey church is open to the public, who are welcome to attend services. It is advisable to telephone in advance to check times (☎ (01983) 882420). Men who wish to get away from their hectic lifestyles can volunteer for a retreat at Quarr.

A little further on, in a field beside the footpath to Binstead and Ryde, is the site of the Cistercian abbey of **Quarr**, founded in 1132 by Baldwin de Redvers, originally as a Savignac house. It was once the leading religious institution on the Island and the pre-eminent place of burial for the local nobility. During the Middle Ages, it acquired extensive lands, endowments and revenues, including numerous granges and farms on the Island.

Dissolved in 1536, much of the stone went to build the forts at Cowes and Yarmouth. Excavations in 1891 revealed the ground plan of the original monastery, but today all that remains above ground are a few isolated walls and a storehouse retained as a barn. Cottages nearby contain features made from salvaged materials.

Binstead church was founded in about 1170 apparently because the abbot of Quarr was fed up with the locals annoying the monks. Despite restoration in 1844 and a serious fire in 1969, many Early English features remain, together with the usual memorials and some interesting tombstones in the churchyard. There is also some fine panelling and stone carving and the grotesque Binstead 'idol' over a Norman archway in the south wall.

From Binstead there is a path through woodlands and past a golf course to a quiet beach. Just southwest of Binstead, **Brickfields** has more than a hundred animals from Shire horses to miniature ponies as well as a farm and pets' corner. The racing pigs run daily during the season. It is an excellent excursion for all the family and riding lessons can be booked for all age groups.

A 1920s guidebook once said that Ryde was a town 'where no discriminating tourist will linger'. This is a mistake, for the town has a great deal more to offer beyond its immediate appearance. **Ryde** is the largest town on the Island, with a population of 24,000, and indeed some visitors hardly venture beyond it, particularly the large number of day-trippers.

It does have an air of faded Regency and Victorian grandeur and the atmosphere differs slightly from elsewhere on the Island. This may be because Portsmouth is clearly visible on the mainland just a nine-minute hovercraft ride away. Also, Ryde has a very high level year-round residency and overall is less affected by seasonal changes in income and population.

Ryde comes from a local word *ride* or *rithe* meaning a small stream. There is archaeological and documentary evidence of continuity of settlement from the Neolithic period and late Bronze Age onwards. In medieval times, it was a fishing, trading and ferry settlement, but was burnt by the French in 1377. Subsequently, two settlements, Upper Ryde, along the High Street, and Lower Ryde, along the foreshore, grew up.

In 1780, Union Street was laid out by William Player to join the two communities and to create a Regency watering place to rival Brighton. By the late 1820s, fashionable Ryde was the most rapidly growing area of the Island with increasing numbers of public buildings and rows of elegant houses. The Town Hall, St Thomas's Church and Brigstocke Terrace date from this period, to be followed by John Lind's classical assembly rooms and market in 1831 and Westmacott's Italianate Royal Victoria Arcade in 1836.

Ryde's skyline is dominated by the 180ft (55m) spire of All Saints'

Brickfields Horsecountry

Working displays and seasonal farming activities; saddlery, gift shop, restaurant and bar
☎ (01983) 566801.

Open: every day all year round.

church, a well-used seamark for ships entering and exiting Portsmouth. Sir George Gilbert Scott designed the predominantly alabaster and marble church to seat 1,300 souls. The spire was added in 1881-2.

The establishment of the Ryde to Ventnor railway line in the 1860s considerably opened up the resorts of the south-east coast and the growing popularity of Cowes led to the steady decline of Ryde as a fashionable resort in its own right.

The pier, built in 1814, for ferry passengers, runs for half a mile (0.8km) into the sea and is the second longest in the country. The first regular ferry service had been inaugurated in 1805 and the pier allowed travellers to disembark from ferries without the inconvenience of riding on a pony and cart across the muddy foreshore. 1817 saw the first steam ferry, but it was not until 1824 that a regular steamer service was instituted, taking thirty-four minutes.

The landward end of the pier is the terminus for bus and coach services to other parts of the Island. The visitor cannot fail to see the assortment of hotels, guesthouses, pubs, cafes, amusement arcades and 'kiss me quick' souvenir shops. The Tourist Information Centre is on the Esplanade at the bottom of Union Street.

The town with its outlying areas has 6 miles (9.6km) of sandy, clean beaches, which are ideal for swimming and, particularly at low tide, for playing. The long seafront esplanade is suitable for walks and there is a host of seasonal attractions, including putting, trampolines, a marina and a canoe lake. In a field by the Esplanade, now the boating lake, the victims of the wreck of the *Royal George*, the flagship of Admiral Kempenfelt, were buried in 1782. There were wives and families on board when she sank in Spithead and at least 800 souls perished. There is a small memorial to the *Royal George* opposite Esplanade Gardens.

Ice Arena and LA Bowl

On the Esplanade is the **Planet Ice Arena and Skating Rink,** which is open for recreational skating all year round and is home to the Wightlink Raiders ice hockey team ☎ (01983) 615155.

Next to the Ice Arena is **LA Bowl** – a 22-lane bowling alley.

☎ (01983) 617070.

The Ryde Road train service operates from Easter to October following a route via Puckpool Park – Appley Park – Boating lake – Upper Town via George St and returning via Union Street. This novel form of transport saves hiking up Union Street to the top of town.

On the eastern side of Ryde is **Appley Park,** formerly a private estate built by a blacksmith called Boyce, who was suspected of making his money in smuggling. It has ornamental gardens, woods and a pitch and putt.

Further along the coast **Puckpool Park** stands on the site of a former battery. Now it is a well-laid out park with a bowling green, tennis courts, crazy golf, putting green, swings and a play area. There are also an aquarium, an aviary and some quiet wooded walks, together with a small wireless museum.

Shopping in Ryde requires an element of exploration. Union Street, once full of elegant townhouses but now housing traditional and more unusual shops, runs from the Esplanade into the High Street and beyond. Half way up Union Street on

The beach at Ryde

the right hand side is the Royal Victoria Arcade, saved by conservationists in the 1970s. One can detect its former grandeur when looking up at the ceiling, but the shops do not match its nineteenth century glory. It is full of small bric-a-brac shops, trendy handbag and sweater outlets and second hand bookshops, some worth a browse, particularly Pickwick's second-hand paperbacks and some of the more genuinely antique bric-a-brac shops.

Outside, Cross Street runs off to the left and boasts several bookshops, including Heritage Antiquarian Books and Prints and one of the best stocked and staffed clothes shops on the Island, Elizabeth Pack.

Just off Union Street at its junction with the High Street is **St Thomas's Church**. Built in 1827 it is now leased to Isle of Wight Council and open to the public on weekdays only. Further up the High Street through the main shopping precinct is St Mary's Roman Catholic church. Built in early English style it was designed by Joseph Hansom, the creator of the Hansom Cab, in 1844-46.

Ryde Theatre on Lind Street stands on the site of an old theatre. Here Mrs Jordan appeared for the last time in England and Ellen Terry for the first time on the stage, as a child, playing Puck in 'A Midsummer Night's Dream'.

On the outskirts of Ryde you will find **Waltzing Waters**, a forty-minute show with moving fountains and waterspouts synchronised with waltzes and music of all kinds. Close by is the **Busy Bee Garden Centre** with its large coffee shop. ☎ 01983 811096.

Waltzing Waters

A3055, just south of Ryde
Aqua Theatre at the Westridge Centre
☎ (01983) 811333.

Rosemary Vineyard is on a 30-acre (12-hectare) site that was planted in 1986 at 60ft (18m) above sea level. There are tours and tastings available and a small shop selling wine and other related products. The Vine Leaf is open for snacks. In fine weather, visitors can follow the sign-posted vineyard trail.

Rosemary Vineyard

Smallbrook Lane, just south of Ryde
☎ (01983) 811084.
Open: all year except Sundays in winter.

Smallbrook Stadium

Just south of Rosemary Vineyard
Weekly premier league speedway programme in the summer
☎ (01983) 811180.

Smallbrook railway junction is located nearby and is the interchange for the main railway line but NOTE that it is not possible to join trains here, except by the Isle of Wight Steam Railway.

SEAVIEW
TO BEMBRIDGE

The quieter and more exclusive resort of Seaview is about 2.5 miles (4km) east of Ryde, along the Duver Road. The sea-front provides uninterrupted and extensive views of Spithead, the shipping activity in the Solent and the scenery of the mainland. It is a popular summer sailing centre and there are two sandy bays suitable for bathing in water that is noticeably clear. Nearby Priory Bay, beyond Horestone Point, and Nettlestone are less busy and St Helen's can be reached along the sands at low tide.

Bembridge Life Boat Station

The nearby **Flamingo Park**, over-looking the Solent, with over a hundred flamingos, also has a colony of Humboldt penguins and one of the largest waterfowl collections in the country. There is a gift shop, café and water displays.

Flamingo Park

Springvale, Seaview
Open: 10am-5pm daily, Easter to September,
10am-4pm daily in October
☎ (01983) 612153.

In the area are many footpaths and two extremely pleasant walking routes along the coast. One goes to Ryde initially along the Duver Road to Puckpool Park and then along the sands (at low tide) or along the sea-wall. The other takes the Coastal Path which weaves inland to St Helen's and takes in the Duver, a spit of sand and shingle projecting into Bembridge Harbour.

St Helen's is a scattered village grouped loosely around an open green. In medieval times, a Cluniac Priory stood near the old church. Only part of the square tower of this church remains as a sea-mark and a

new church of 1717 was constructed on the road to Nettlestone.

In the late eighteenth century, the village, with a population of 2,000, thrived as a supply port for sailing men-of-war, which lay off-shore in St Helen's Roads, to avoid being trapped in Spithead or Portsmouth by adverse winds. It was also a good place to ensure pressed men did not desert and, sheltered from the westerly winds, to conduct gunnery and sail handling training. Stones from the old church were used to scrape the upper decks of the ships of dirt and salt, hence the expression 'holystoning', or polishing, the decks. Offshore is St Helen's fort, one of Palmerston's artillery forts of 1860, to which an annual walk takes place at low tide.

Palmerston's Solent Forts

Wightbyte

The four forts that can be seen in the Solent were built in the 1860s to defend Portsmouth and the Solent against possible attack. In the Crimean war, the Royal Navy had been surprised by the effectiveness of the Russian forts at Sebastopol so plans for fortifications at key ports and points along the south and east coasts of England were drafted. As Britain's pre-eminent naval port, it was considered that Portsmouth needed an all round defence, and a comprehensive system of forts and artillery batteries was built in the 1860s around Gosport, Portsmouth and the Isle of Wight to strengthen existing arrangements at a cost of roughly £1.5 million.

The four Solent sea forts were built to cover the deep-water passage through Spithead. The two largest are No Man's Land and Horse Sand, with the smaller, Spitbank and St Helen's, and were all constructed 1868-71 with a complex layered structure of armour and heavy masonry on granite foundations.

Other forts in the system can be seen at intervals along the crest of Portsdown Hill above Portsmouth. Around the Island, other traces of the system may be seen, particularly guarding the Needles' Channel *(Fort Victoria, Fort Albert, Golden Hill* and a host of minor batteries on the Freshwater Peninsula) and at Sandown, Bembridge, Yaverland and Puckpool, protecting the eastern approaches to the Island.

Oasis

Carpenter's Road, St Helens
Unusual shop, full of delightful knick-knacks, described by the proprietors as 'novel, inspirational, bizarre and amusing' from all over the world
☎ (01983) 613760.
Web-site: www.oasis-iow.com

Bembridge Down offers one of the best and most varied views on the Island, from the Hampshire coast all the way round to **Dunnose Head**, with **Bembridge** in the fore-ground. Next to the easterly car park, there is an

Continued on page 32...

Shipwreck and Maritime Museum

Sherbourne Street, Bembridge
Open: 10am-5pm daily, April to October

☎ (01983) 872223.

Visitors will see on maps and on the ground that the Island was once covered with an extensive railway network. The first line was started in 1859 from Cowes to Newport and by 1900 there were 55 miles (89km) of track, with an extension to Ryde Pier Head to connect with the ferries. In the 1930s, on each Saturday in summer, 36,000 passengers would pass through Ryde Pier and a train would leave every 10 minutes.

After nationalisation in 1948 and increasing competition from road transport, the branch lines ceased to be economic and by 1960 all but the 8.5-mile (13.6km) section between Ryde Pier Head and Shanklin had been shut. Since 1966 the service has been modernized using electrified ex-Underground stock. The line – the Island Line – currently has official recognition as Britain's most punctual and reliable rail service.

The small village of **Havenstreet** was a haven when Wootton creek extended further inland. Today, it is the headquarters and maintenance depot of the **Isle of Wight Steam Railway**, which operates a 5.2-mile (8.3km) line between Wootton and Smallbrook Junction, with inter-mediate stations at Havenstreet and Ashey, principally with the support of volunteers.

After the last steam service on the Island, a group of enthusiasts formed the Wight Locomotive Society in 1966 to preserve one of the surviving locomotives. The 2-mile (3.2km) stretch of track

Isle of Wight Steam Railway

between Wootton and Havenstreet was leased from 1971 and acquisitions of locomotives, rolling stock and buildings from all over the Island since then have subtained rapid development.

Havenstreet Railway

Nowadays, the line connects at Smallbrook Junction with the Island Line and regular passenger and themed services are operated along the whole preserved section, using a combination of Victorian and Edwardian engines and carriages. Trains run about every hour during the day in summer and the rural stations themselves are delightful and very evocative, having incorporated structures rescued from other long lost stations on the Island. ☎ (01983) 884343

Real enthusiasts wishing to explore the old tracks should start at Havenstreet Station itself where there is a well-stocked souvenir and railway memorabilia shop and an interesting collection of local railway items. It is also the best place to see the engines and rolling stock, although visits to the depot itself are not permitted. Visitors can gain an appreciation of the network at its height and an understanding of its history. Nearby, Ashey is a good place for ramblers and cyclists to alight, by request, but it is not accessible by car. Similarly, access at Smallbrook Junction is only by rail.

The Ryde Bookshop in the High Street specialises in railways and transport. Jeff Vinter's book, *Railway Walks (GWR and SR)* (Alan Sutton) gives an excellent potted history of the network and detailed instructions on how to find vestiges of the lines and original buildings. In addition, there are four short walks, which take in the old railway track beds and which are clearly marked on the Ordnance Survey Outdoor Leisure Map 29:

Cowes to Newport (4.5 miles/7.2km) – This popular route starts at the end of Arctic Road, Cowes, and runs along the west bank of the Medina. It has a layer of tarmac, making it suitable for walkers, cyclists and wheelchairs.

Yarmouth to Freshwater (2.5 miles/4km) – This is a wonderful walk along the eastern bank of the River Yar, returning to Yarmouth on the western side or continuing into Freshwater itself.

Shanklin to Wroxall (2.5 miles/4km) – This walk starts just south of Shanklin station and winds around St Martin's Down. A picturesque and most rewarding return is easily made along the Worsley Trail from Wroxall.

Sandown to Horringford (3 miles/4.8km) – Start at Sandown station and follow the Nunwell trail along Golf Links Road and Longwood road 880yds/ 800m to some reservoirs. Here the old track bed is visible as a path heading off to the left alongside the golf course. The path heads via Alverstone to Horringford.

obelisk commemorating the first Earl of Yarborough, who was the first Commodore of the Royal Yacht Squadron. He paid his yachting crews extra wages if they would voluntarily conform to the regulations of the Royal Navy; at that time, these included flogging for various infractions of discipline.

Culver Cliff (National Trust), a striking mass of chalk and flint, defines the northern end of **Sandown Bay** and fronts Bembridge Down. From the northern end of Sandown seafront, it can be reached by means of a cliff path on foot and the return trip is about 5 miles (8km). Others may wish to walk along the sands at the base of the cliffs, at appropriate levels of tide, and enjoy the foreshore and rock pools. The cliff is approachable by road through **Yaverland** by continuing beyond the fort on the summit of Bembridge Down.

Bembridge and St Helens used to be situated on either side of the entrance to Brading Haven and Bembridge itself was virtually cut off from the rest of the Island. Eventually a mile long embankment was built from St Helens to Bembridge to keep out the sea. A railway link was established and the village, supposedly the largest in the country, grew in size and popularity.

Bembridge is today a trendy yachting and residential area. The rim of today's shallow haven is fronted with houseboats and other nautical paraphernalia. The prestigious Bembridge Sailing Club, founded in 1886, has an interesting, self-satisfied clubhouse fronting the sea along the embankment. Bembridge is in fact home to two sailing clubs – the other is the Brading Haven Yacht Club – and both clubs host sailing activities all year. A busy marina operates at St Helens and a number of commercial fishing-craft work the harbour; fishing trips can be booked.

The **RNLI Station** at Lane End operates an offshore and a D-Class inshore lifeboat. The lifeboat station

Bembridge Windmill (NT)

Open: 10am-4.30pm daily end of March to October, (closed Saturdays except July and August)
☎ (01983) 873945.

is usually open to the public during the summer for free guided tours subject to manning and operational requirements.

Bembridge Village has a wide variety of shops, pubs and restaurants. One of the main attractions is the privately owned **Shipwreck and Maritime Museum** overflowing with artefacts recovered from local waters. It is also home to a unique collection of ship models and tells the story of past and present Bembridge lifeboats.

A display of Bembridge past and present can be seen in the Roy Baker Heritage Society collection and visitors should check opening arrangements on ☎ (01983) 873100.

Just outside the village is the last remaining windmill on the Island that dates from 1700 and commands spectacular views of the surrounding countryside. **Bembridge Windmill** (National Trust) has been restored and contains a complete set of wooden machinery and gearing, most of it original.

Bembridge Airport, the base for Britten-Norman, builders of the *Islander* and *Defender* aircraft, has the only all-weather runway and facilities on the Island. The Schneider Trophy weekend takes place every year in July and attracts many visitors to an airborne activities programme organised at the airport.

From Bembridge Point, there is a remarkable sea view and at low tide a long stretch of firm sand, ideal for children and adults to play on. Under Tyne with its sand and shingle is the only place to bathe. There is a cheerful, scenic coast walk from Bembridge to Sandown (5 miles/8km), via the Foreland, Whitecliff Bay, Culver Cliff and Bembridge Down.

BRADING

Brading used to send two members to parliament, but has been left high and dry, both by history and by reclamation of the once navigable Brading Haven in 1878. Today, it is easy for travellers to miss Brading, but it is worth stopping. There are a number of attractions, not least the church, a line of old cottages (mostly with nineteenth-century frontages) in the High Street, and the water meadows along the banks of the River Yar.

Quay Lane, between the church and the museum gives access to the water meadows and an excellent walk to Bembridge, via its windmill. Brading is also a convenient centre for walking the Downs, with easy access to Brading, Ashey, Mersley and Arreton Downs and elsewhere, all at an altitude of between 300 and 400ft (92m and 122m).

Lilliput Antique Doll and Toy Museum

Brading High Street, Has over 2,000 exhibits – dolls, dolls' houses, traditional toys and teddy bears
www.lilliputmuseum.com
☎ (01983) 407231.
Open: 10am-
5pm daily,
all year.

A Saxon church may have stood on the site of St Mary's, but the current church dates from 1150-1250. It has a host of interesting features: a tower built on piers, a thirteenth-century font, the Oglander and de Aula family chapels and some evocative stained glass. The Oglander table-tombs and memorials, commemorating probably the most notable Island family, from nearby **Nunwell**, are remarkable, including one with a '*Pieta*' by Francia.

Nunwell House

About a mile west of Brading
Historic former seat of the Oglander family at least since the reign of Henry I (1100-1135). This Jacobean and Georgian building has a collection of period furniture
☎ (01983) 407240.

Open: House and Garden open July to September on Monday, Tuesday & Wednesday afternoons. Please ring to double-check.
The garden may be open
at other times in support
of charity.

Next to the church is the Old Town Hall which houses stocks and a whipping post. The village lock-up was also in the building. Opposite in the old sixteenth century rectory is the **Brading Experience** which has themed exhibits based on historic scenes and strange tales from the Island's past as well as a Chamber of Horrors. The World of Wheels is a recent addition to this attraction and is in an adjacent purpose built engine shed.

The Brading Experience

Brading. Car park to the rear.
www.bradingtheexperience.co.uk
☎ (01983) 407286.
Open: all
year round.
Entrance
charge.

The first class **Brading Roman Villa** once stood on one of the inlets formed by Brading Haven and was probably an important agricultural centre. The villa survived into the fifth century and the excellent museum covering the remains includes the main rooms of a substantial house, with detailed mosaics and an award winning exhibition. The car park area is a great place for a picnic close to the sites of Roman outbuildings and a Roman well holds a sinister secret.

Morton Manor, just south of Brading, is family run and offers a warm welcome and unexpected pleasures. The manor was originally built in 1249 and was enlarged with a Tudor longhouse, before a substantial remodelling in 1680 and re-

Brading Roman Villa

Open daily March-October 9.30am-6pm Nov –
Feb 10am-4pm. Good coffee shop open every day
10.30am-4pm' www.bradingromanvilla.org.uk
or ☎ 01983 406223.

furbishment in the Georgian period.

The immaculately maintained gardens are a delight and were winners of the Isle of Wight in Bloom Award from 1995-7. Based around Elizabethan sunken gardens and a combination of formal and informal settings, they are alive with colour amid parkland, woodland and terraces. Attached is a vineyard producing predominantly white table wine where visitors can view the winemaking process on video and sample the wines.

The Downs at Adgestone

Morton Manor

House, gardens, tearoom and shop.
☎ (01983) 406168.
Open Sunday to Friday from Easter until October 10am – 5.30pm (Last admission 4.30pm)

Adgestone Vineyard

Just south of Brading
Produces more than 40,000 bottles of white wine (three varieties) per year. A new red wine is being developed. There is a small shop, café and tasting room ☎ (01983) 402503. Open: 10am-5pm daily, Easter to October. Limited winter opening.

Vineyard Walk

Distance: approximately 5 miles (8km)

The close proximity of the three main Island vineyards – Rosemary, Adgestone and Morton Manor – offers the opportunity to base a walk on the vineyard theme. Start at Ryde St John's station and take the Nunwell Trail (follow the red flashes on the signposts) through the suburb of Oakfield. Go along the railway and just north of Smallbrook Junction, turn right over the railway and take Smallbrook Lane to Rosemary Vineyard.

Leaving the vineyard, turn right and continue up the lane, passing a stadium on your left. Turn left at the crossroads onto Ashey Road and pick up the trail again leading off to the left after about 550 yds (500 m). Continue across open country until you hit a small road near Hardingshute Farm and turn right. Cross West Lane and walk towards Nunwell Farm, with Nunwell House visible to your left. Take a sharp right turn, skirting a small wood, then – particular care is needed here – turn sharp left, leaving the Nunwell trail, onto a bridlepath. After about 220yds (200m) fork right and ascend Brading Down for a wonderful view to the south.

Descend into Adgestone and the vineyard is on your right as you hit the first minor road. A walk along the Lower Adgestone Road will bring you to Morton Manor. To return to Ryde St John's, walk from Morton Manor towards the Yarbridge crossroads and pick up the footpath on the east side of the railway. Follow this to Brading station and catch the train.

Yaverland lies between Brading and Sandown. The church was built in about 1150 as a chapel of the de Aula family, which owned the manor house at a time when Yaverland was a tidal island. It became a parish church in the fif- teenth century and was heavily restored in 1889. However, many of its original, particularly Norman, features have been retained. The privately owned Jacobean Manor House is not open to the public.

SANDOWN

Sitting in its 6-mile (10km) wide bay, between the chalk of Culver Cliff and the ruddy Dunnose Head, Sandown is the Island's premier holiday resort. The red brick town is somewhat overpopulated with hotels and guesthouses but it has a wonderful sandy beach unencumbered by rocks and pebbles and a pier. It does get very busy in season and is especially geared for entertaining families and children. However, this functional and busy seasonal resort can in winter look abandoned, run down and distinctly sad.

Sandown Bay from the Downs

Sandown shares the bay with its posher neighbour, Shanklin, together with a sheltered south-easterly aspect and the sunshine record for the south of England. Indeed, they are administratively and psychologically linked; even in 1920, Ward Lock's guide book observed, 'The twin towns of Sandown and Shanklin share this bay between them. There is every indication that their rivalry will one day cease by the simple process of amalgamation'.

In 1537, Sir Richard Worsley of Appuldurcombe, Captain of the Island, built a castle at Sandham on behalf of Henry VIII to protect the vulnerable east coast from invaders. This fort fell into the sea in about 1630 and a successor was demolished in the nineteenth-century. In 1861 work began on a new Sandown fort, which was complete by 1866, but is now the Isle of Wight Zoo.

The town's popularity grew as a resort in company with Shanklin and Ventnor during the mid-Victorian era, particularly after the construction of the railway from Ryde and after 1867 when Dr Henry Maund extolled the virtues of the local air and low mortality rate. Lodging houses proliferated and in 1874 four European monarchs stayed (ironically, the same year that Karl Marx stayed in Ventnor).

Sandown Pier first opened in 1878 and is 1,000 feet (305m) long, having been lengthened in 1895 and a landing stage added to give access by steamer. The large **pier pavilion** was built at a cost of £26,000 in 1934 and now houses an all year round entertainment complex. The view from the seaward end of the pier is exhilarating.

The esplanade is well supplied with bars, cafés, bingo halls and amusement arcades including the **Wight City Leisure Complex** on Culver Parade. There is a market on the car park of the White City Leisure Complex every Monday during the main season.

At the Yaverland end of the town are long and short, pitch and putt courses (**Brown's**) plus the famous zoo housed in Granite Fort. At the northern end of the esplanade are Sandham Grounds, home to a variety of amusements including putting, tennis and bowls. Nearby is an 18 inch (46cm) deep canoe lake. **Sandown Zoo and Big Cat Sanctuary** houses tigers, black panthers, leopards and pumas. There are

Wightbyte — Visitors

Charles Darwin began writing the work popularly known as *The Origin of Species* in Sandown and Sir Isaac Pitman formulated his famous system of shorthand. Lewis Carroll, John Keats, George Eliot and Henry Longfellow were all appreciative visitors.

Sandown Bay with Culver Cliff in the distance

Wightbyte

Shipwreck

In 1878, the passage of the 900 ton, 26 gun frigate *Eurydice* on her return from a West Indies training cruise was witnessed by the 4 year old Winston Churchill and his nurse, who hurried home to avoid a storm. The ship subsequently went down in a squall in the same storm and, of the 300 crew, only two were saved. Seven of the drowned were buried in the churchyard of Christchurch, Sandown. A memorial reads, "Sacred to the memory of seven brave men of Her Majesty's Navy, who lie buried here after having first found a watery grave on Sunday March 24th 1878 when *HMS Eurydice* foundered in a terrific squall off Sandown Bay".

many other exotic species such as lemurs, monkeys, reptiles, birds, insects and giant spiders.

Sandown Zoo

Yaverland, nr Sandown
Facilities include a large car park, gift shop and snack bar.
☎ (01983) 403883.
 Open 10am-6pm daily from April to September and 10am-4pm daily mid-Feb-March and Oct. www.isleofwightzoo.com

In 2001 a brand new all weather, purpose built interactive attraction known as Dinosaur Isle opened on Culver Parade and incorporated the geology museum previously located in Sandown library. Life size dinosaur models are featured in their natural landscape as well as a display of fossils found on the Isle of Wight.

At the southern end of the esplanade is a clifftop walk to Shanklin with access to **Battery Gardens** on the site of an old fortlet. Dotto cars operate in both Sandown and Shanklin.

Lake is a residential area sandwiched between Sandown and Shanklin struggling to retain its identity. An early twentieth-century

Sandown Pier

☎ (01983) 404122
www.sandown-pier.com
Open daily 9am –11pm (10pm in winter) Bowling, adventure golf and children's play area.

visitor noted gloomily, 'Lake, nearly midway between Sandown and Shanklin, already affords a link and it will soon be difficult for the stranger to say where Sandown and Shanklin begin'.

Dinosaur Isle

Interactive Dinosaur and Geology Museum Tel 01983 404344 0r www.dinosaurisle.com.
Open daily all year except 25 & 26 Dec & 1 Jan. Nov-March 10am-4pm (last entry 3pm); April-Oct 10am-6pm and 5pm in Oct (last entry 5pm and 4pm in Oct)

SHANKLIN

The old village of Shanklin, with its thatched cottages and 400-year old Crab Inn, was built at the top of a chine, which winds from the 100ft (30.5m) cliff-top to the sea, and to the south of the present town. The church, another of Norman origin, had virtually a complete makeover in 1852 and was significantly extended. There is a variety of souvenir and gift shops while walkers will find paths radiating inland and up on to the Downs.

Shanklin Old Village

In 1545, the **Shanklin Chine** was the scene of a battle to repel French raiders, during which their commander was killed. It now contains waterfalls, trees and lush vegetation to which footpaths and walkways allow access for visitors. A Heritage Centre tells the history of the Chine in words and pictures.

Shanklin Chine

☎ (01983) 866432.
Open: 10am-5pm daily, Easter to late-May and mid-September to end of October; 10am-10pm daily, late-May to mid-September. Open subject to weather conditions.

To the south is **Rylstone Gardens,** an extremely well-tended and picturesque location with lawns, conifers and shrubs. The views are extensive and the gardens lead to Appley Green (more views) and the beach.

The esplanade and a sandy beach tend to be, but are not always, quieter than Sandown. There is a lift between the cliff top and the sea front. It has a putting green, crazy golf and the usual run of amusements, arcades and children's temptations. For adults, there is a broad selection of pubs, eateries and restaurants as well as live entertainment in season. **Shanklin Theatre** has up to eight different shows per week in high season.

From the old church, a well-marked path leads to **Shanklin Down** and then **St Boniface Down,** at 783ft (239m) the highest point on the Island, and the pleasant, usually bracing climb is worth the effort. Another walk, over 3 miles (4.8km), to Ventnor, takes in Luc-combe Chine, the **Landslip** and Bonchurch.

Once in Luccombe, there is a pleasant walk to **Luccombe Common** and **Nansen Hill,** from which there is an extensive view of Sandown Bay. A further walk extends to Luccombe Chine, which as far as Dunnose Head gives access to the Landslip. This is a well sign-posted jumble of rocks and vegetation, with footpaths and routes of varying difficulty, ideal for exploring and for getting down to the caves of Luccombe and **Monks Bay.** The more adventurous can enjoy a scramble down the steps of the Devil's Chimney and other clefts; others might want the calm of the gardens on the Upper Landslip.

Shanklin's pier was severely damaged in the hurricane of 1987 and after further deterioration was demolished in 1993. It had been the base for PLUTO, the PipeLine Under The Ocean, which supplied fuel oil to the Allied Expeditionary Force during the D-day landings in 1944.

VENTNOR

Ventnor has merged with the older village of Bonchurch which still retains some charm with its pond and church. Its upper part offers probably one of the best views on the Island. At its centre is a remarkable shrub and tree-lined pond, which was given to the village as a memorial to his wife by H de Vere Stacpoole, author of *The Blue Lagoon* and the poem, *In a Bonchurch Garden*. He was one of many members of Victorian society who chose to live in Bonchurch, including Tennyson, Macaulay, and Elisabeth Sewell.

The charming, simple old church of St Boniface, peacefully set among trees and roses, was probably built around 1070 on a site of early Saxon foundation. Houses nearby also have their literary associations: the poet

Swinburne was born at East Dene and Dickens lived for a while at Winterbourne, writing part of *David Copperfield* here. Swinburne is buried along with other members of his family at the newer church of St Boniface, built in 1847-8.

Facing south and in a sheltered position, Ventnor grew rapidly as a health resort in the 1840s, as visitors sought to take advantage of the mild winter climate and sea air. On a one in four incline to a height of 800ft (244m), it is built on a series of terraces, which have been likened by some to rows of seats in a theatre. These are supplemented by flights of stairs and zig-zag roads which may deter all but the most determined explorer on foot.

Its major buildings and numerous churches all date from the mid-Victorian era and there are antique and other interesting shops. Ventnor has many of the attractions associated with the twentieth-century tourist boom, most of which are close to sea level, but the quaintness of the town prevents this becoming overpowering. A Victorian style bandstand has been built where the old pier stood and evening concerts take place in the summer.

Local brew

Wightbyte

The local Ventnor Brewery has been brewing beer since 1840 and uses the distinctive St Boniface Down spring water in its process. After an agreement of 1850, the brewery was granted unlimited access to the water for 6 old pence (2.5 new pence) a year for 1,000 years. An enemy bomb destroyed the brewhouse in 1943 and killed the owner, but it was restored in 1953.

Ventnor's sea-front is divided by a 'cascade'. On the eastern side, there is a canoe lake, paddling pool and a promenade with gardens and the usual amenities. The western portion is dominated by a beach, which is sand and fine shingle with some rocky outcrops. The family firm of Blake has fished from the beach for five generations and still sells to local restaurants and pubs.

One of Ventnor's most attractive and popular features is its Park, which takes up most of its southern slope. Amid the plants and paths, there is enough space for visitors to enjoy privacy while enjoying the commanding views.

Botanic Gardens

The Botanic Gardens, which benefit from the sub-tropical climatic effects of Ventnor's situation, contain over 10,000 plants and 4,000 species, some of which might seem more at home in a Mediterranean environment. Formerly the site of the Royal National Hospital for Diseases of the Chest founded in 1861, the 22-acre (9-hectare) gardens take advantage of the terraces of the former hospital grounds and are open during daylight hours all year
☎ (01983) 855397.

12
60

Ventnor Museums

Museum of Smuggling History
Botanic Gardens
☎ (01983) 853677.

Longshoreman's Museum
The Esplanade
Describes Ventnor's nautical history (photographs, engravings and models)
☎ (01983) 853176.

Ventnor Heritage Centre and Local History Museum
Spring Hill off the High Street
☎ (01983) 855407.

IOW Coastal Visitors' Centre
Dudley Road
☎ (01983) 855400.

The Undercliff, a 7-mile (11.2km) long landslip, forms a remarkable inland cliff about 600yds (550m) wide between Blackgang and Luccombe. Recurrent slides and falls have been caused by the unusual geological structure, the action of weather and the presence of numerous streams. The main culprit is the combination of chalk and greensand layers overlying the 'Blue Slipper' clay.

Most significant activity occurred in prehistoric times, but there have been memorable slips in 1799, 1818 and in 1928, when a major section of the coast road was lost. In February 1995, 1.5 million tonnes of rock and debris crashed into the sea between Bonchurch and Dunnose.

The whole area is rich in plant and vegetation, providing a ready habitat for birds and other local wildlife. It is also a favourite stop-over for migrating species. Numerous paths give access along its whole length and exploration is highly recommended for adults and children, particularly the uninterrupted stretch between the Botanic Gardens and Blackgang (5 miles/8km).

St Lawrence is part of the ribbon development to the south-west of Ventnor and can be reached either along the main road or the Undercliff. The tiny, evocative church is off the beaten track and set in woods, but fully repays the effort of a visit. It dates from the twelfth-century and originally measured only 25 x 11 x 6ft (7.6 x 3.4 x 1.8m) high (up to its beams). Until 1842, when a new chancel extended its length by 15ft (4.6m), it was the smallest parish church in England. There is a newer church designed by Gilbert Scott and built in 1878 with pre-Raphaelite stained glass salvaged from the Royal National Hospital.

Nearby is Lisle Combe, bought by the poet Alfred Noyes in the Thirties. It is still owned by his family and run as a farmhouse B & B (www.lislecombe.co.uk) Guests have access to the adjacent farm.

Located close to St Lawrence Undercliff in a converted farm building is the internationally renowned studio of Isle of Wight glass where glassmaking is demonstrated.

Isle of Wight Studio Glass

St Lawrence
Tel 01983 853526.
Open Mon – Fri 10am-4pm Oct – Easter except Christmas Holiday period. Open daily 9am-5pm Easter – Oct.

INLAND

Newchurch, with its panoramic views on the end of a long escarpment, retains a rural, attractive atmosphere and stands above the eastern Yar river valley. Its church, dating from Norman times and containing a number of curiosities, principally a tower clad in eighteenth-century weather boarding, has the best view of all.

The village has long been the centre of the Island's horticulture and today has several nurseries and garden centres. More recently, garlic, asparagus and sweetcorn have been farmed and an annual two-day garlic festival takes place on the third weekend in August, which provides substantial financing for local projects.

Newchurch has good connections and opportunities for walking and cycling with many footpaths, bridleways and cycle tracks. Wildlife enthusiasts will be able to visit the nearby **Alverstone Nature Reserve**, which has red squirrels. Alverstone itself has an old mill and some pleasant cottages, with opportunities for refreshments.

Just to the south is Queen's Bower, where there is access to **Borthwood Copse**, whose paths thread through quiet and dense woodland, thickly set with wild flowers. A further walk to Brading Down (near Adgestone Vineyard) allows a stroll along a butterfly footpath where the Glanville fritillary butterfly, unique to the Island, can be found.

Amazon World, adjacent to Thompson's Café, Plant and Garden Centre, is a great all weather attraction, as well as being an enjoyable educational experience. Exotic birds fly freely among the lush tropical growth where marmosets and monkeys play. Amazon World recreates the story of the rainforest and portrays the environment of endangered species and life in the jungle.

Amazon World

Watery Lane, Newchurch
Includes outside animal enclosures and children's play area
☎ (01983) 867122.
Open:
all year.

Wroxall's hitherto agricultural character was transformed by the coming of the railway, which Lord Yarborough of Appuldurcombe would not allow across his land. Consequently, a tunnel of 1,301 yds (1,190m) was cut through St Boniface Down and Wroxall's cottages expanded to house the workers. The village, in a hollow of the Downs, has walks in all directions.

Wroxall's main attraction is **Appuldurcombe House**, a roofless, but impressive shell with grounds landscaped by Capability Brown. Its history mainly revolves around the Worsley family, which came from Lancashire. James Worsley was a page to King Henry VII and a companion to the future King Henry VIII. In 1509, Worsley was knighted and made Captain of the Isle of Wight. He married Ann Leigh, the heiress of Appuldurcombe, and founded a dynasty, which would dominate Island politics and life for three centuries.

The original house was demol-ished and a Palladian mansion of 1701 built in its place. In 1855, when the estate was sold, the house became successively a hotel, a school and finally a temporary refuge for Benedictine monks during the building of Quarr Abbey. From 1909 it decayed rapidly and today it is maintained by English Heritage.

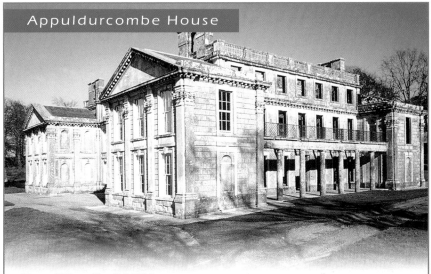

Appuldurcombe House

West of Wroxall, off B3327

An **Owl and Falconry Centre** in the laundry and brewhouse with regular flying displays
☎ (01983) 852484.

Open: 10am-4pm daily May to September; 10am-3pm mid Feb-April & October.

Isle of Wight Donkey Sanctuary

On the outskirts of Wroxall on the road to Godshill is the Isle of Wight Donkey Sanctuary. Over 200 donkeys have been rescued and given a permanent home by a registered charity that subsists entirely on voluntary donations
☎ (01983) 852693.

Whitwell, behind St Lawrence, is remarkable for its double-naved church that has been formed by the incorporation of two medieval chapels built exactly side by side by different lords. Nearby, **Nettlecombe Farm** ☎ (01983) 730783 has three commercial lakes for coarse angling.

The central part of the Island is dominated by the valley of the Medina, with Cowes at its mouth, and the pivotal position of its administrative capital, Newport. Its historic significance is emphasised by the site of the key royal castle of Carisbrooke and the legacy of the Victorian era centred on Osborne.

The influence and involvement of Queen Victoria is everywhere apparent, from memorials by loyal subjects to personal initiatives by the Queen-Empress herself in the life and character of the community. Further south and stretching to St Catherine's Point, are unspoilt villages, open downland and spectacular views.

COWES

Comprising East and West Cowes, linked by a chain floating bridge across the Medina estuary, Cowes lives off its reputation as one of the world's top yachting venues, in particular the prestige associated with the annual 'Cowes' week and as the home of the Royal Yacht Squadron. Facing directly onto Southampton Water, it is also the entry port for visitors arriving from Southampton.

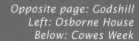

Opposite page: Godshill
Left: Osborne House
Below: Cowes Week

The first recorded use of the name *Cows* was in 1414 and possibly referred to two sandbanks, which lay off the mouth of the Medina. However, a settlement had existed at East Cowes at least from the thirteenth-century, and this was one of the three main recognised ports of the Island a century later with the name of Shamblord. Its importance as a road-stead and harbour was such that Henry VIII built two forts on either

side of the mouth of the river to guard the haven and protect the Island's northern coastline. (Interestingly, the Tudor word for a fortified emplacement was a *cow*.) East Cowes Castle no longer exists but West Cowes castle has been incorporated into the headquarters of the Royal Yacht Squadron.

By the eighteenth-century, shipbuilding, trade and the fashionable pursuit of sea-bathing had increased the prosperity of Cowes significantly. Several large houses were built on both sides of the Medina and Queen Victoria's decision to build at Osborne in 1845 ensured continued growth and prestige for Cowes into the nineteenth-century. The keen interest of the Prince of Wales in yachting and the arrival of the Royal Yacht Club (later Squadron) in 1854 further enhanced Cowes' reputation and attraction. Another of Cowes' claims to fame has been as a home to shipbuilders, primarily J Samuel White and Saunders-Roe, which made high-speed ships, seaplanes and flying boats. Saunders-Roe built Sir Malcolm Campbell's *Bluebird* and developed Sir Christopher Cockerell's hovercraft.

Today, the town lives very much on the tourist and yachting trades, with the focus of much of the entertainment and activity in West Cowes, especially during 'the season', together with the bulk of shops and hotels. The most appealing parts of West Cowes are the open, often bracing, but spectacular sea-front and Prince's Green.

Royal Yacht Squadron at Cowes

Yachting at Cowes

The first attested race at Cowes was in 1788 and, after the Royal Yacht Club was formed in 1815 in London, its first organised events were held in 1826. The Club moved to Cowes in 1854, having adopted the title Royal Yacht Squadron in 1833, under the patronage of William IV. The Prince of Wales (later Edward VII) was for nineteen years the senior flag officer until he became King.

The headquarters of the Royal Yacht Squadron is fronted by 21 brass cannons from the *Royal Adelaide*, the yacht of William IV. These are used to start and finish races. Sailing takes place all the year round, but organised events run mostly between May and September. June sees the Round the Island race when up to 800 boats compete.

During Cowes Week in August the traditional event is the annual Regatta of the Royal Yacht Squadron, but eight other clubs also hold races and regattas.

Around 900 competing boats and 6,000 crew members take part. The Admiral's Cup series is held on alternate (odd) years and the last race of the week is the Fastnet, which ends in Plymouth.

Model Railway Exhibition

The Parade
Model layout plus children's layout. Museum. Well stocked shop for railway buffs. Small admission charge
☎ (01983) 280111. Open all year 11am-5pm Monday to Saturday. Sundays in summer.

Cowes Maritime Museum

Cowes Library, Beckford Road
The Island's maritime history in models, paintings and photographs. Uffa Fox's yachts *Avenger* and *Cowslip*. Free entrance
☎ (01983) 823433. Open 9.30am-5.30pm Mon, Tues & Fri; 11am-7pm Wed; 9.30am-4.30pm Sat; closed Thurs & Sun.

There is a short walk along the old Esplanade in East Cowes to the grounds of Norris Castle, which was built as a mock-Norman residence-cum-folly-cum-farm for Lord Henry Seymour in 1799. In West Cowes, Prince's Esplanade offers a stroll of a mile and a half (2.4km) to Gurnard.

Gurnard is a busy, popular seaside resort with a good beach. It adjoins Northwood Park and House whose 26-acre gardens offer a variety of pleasant walks and sporting amusements. The 15 acre site of the **Isle of Wight Military History Museum** is close by at the former Northwood Camp. (01983) 527411.

Sir Max Aitken Museum

The Sir Max Aitken Museum is in the old Ratsey and Lapthorn sailmakers' loft in the High Street and displays Sir Max Aitken's collection of nautical instruments, paintings and other maritime artefacts.
Small admission charge
☎ (01983) 292191 for details.

AROUND THE MEDINA

Whippingham lies above the River Medina and in medieval times embraced a large area which included Wootton. Despite its early Jutish or Saxon origins, it has no discernible village centre and is very spread out. A footpath leads to the river from where there is a pleasant walk, suitable for birdwatchers, upstream to Newport.

Boating on Wootton Creek

St Mildred's Church is by origin medieval, but was completely rebuilt by John Nash in 1804. As the nearest church to the Osborne estate, this was selected as the site of a church where the Royal Family could worship. Nash's building was demolished and the present extraordinary amalgam of Victorian Gothic, mock medieval and personal whim put up in 1854 and 1861.

Some of the features are remarkable, notably a squat tower with five pinnacles and the royal tombs and memorials, including one to Prince Albert, inside. Indeed, the church has so many Victorian associations and memorabilia that it struggles to maintain its sanctity amid the press of visitors.

St Mildred's Church

Whippingham
Includes Victorian exhibition and tea and souvenir shop. Car & coach park leading to the Orchard and Picnic Area.
Open: 10am-5pm Monday to Friday, Easter to October and during services on Sundays at 11.15am. First-class virtual tour – www.iow.uk.com/whippingham-church.

Sailing legend

Uffa Fox, born in East Cowes in 1898, was a near legendary yachtsman, who in 1928 managed 52 wins out of 57 starts (second in two races and third in three!) in *Avenger*, a 14ft (4m) boat he designed himself. He also designed other racing yachts, including the famous Flying Fifteens and invented the air-deployed lifeboats, which saw service in World War II. Equally famous for his buccaneering lifestyle, he was the doyen of the Isle of Wight yachting scene and died in 1972.

In the churchyard is an iron cross, it marks the grave of Prince Louis of Battenberg, 1st Marquis of Milford Haven, and his wife, Princess Victoria of Hesse, the granddaughter of Queen Victoria. They were the parents of Earl Mountbatten of Burma and grandparents of Prince Philip, the Duke of Edinburgh. By the north wall is the grave of Uffa Fox, the famous yachtsman and boat designer.

Opposite the church are some Almhouses, which were built on the orders of Queen Victoria in 1880 for retired Royal servants. Similarly, Coburg Cottage in Mount Road was built in 1853 and designed by Prince Albert in the style of a Bavarian hunting lodge.

Also in Whippingham is **Barton Manor**. This medieval manor and Jacobean farm was bought by Queen Victoria at the same time as Osborne House and robustly rebuilt by Prince Albert in 1845, to the veiled despair of local and national antiquarians. It was used as an overflow for houseguests and was also the home farm for the Osborne Estate, where additional cooking facilities were used.

Currently in private ownership Barton Manor's 20 acres (8 hectares) of gardens and woodland walks are occasionally opened for themed and charity events. These days are usually advertised in the local press and tourist offices.

Further east near Fishbourne, **Wootton** sits on a tidal estuary and has an attractive, restored church (St Edmund's), with Norman reminders. It and Wootton Bridge are mainly residential, with a beach at Woodside, although modern development and holiday centres crowd the scene. At low tide, the more adventurous will be rewarded with an energetic scramble over the rocks westwards

Butterfly World and Fountain World

Near Wootton Common
Landscaped indoor garden, butterflies from all over the world. Italian and Japanese gardens with water features and fish
☎ (01983) 883430.
Open: 10am-5pm daily, Easter to October. Admission charge.

to King's Quay (about 1.5 miles/ 2.5km return trip).

Just to the south-east, **Firestone Copse** is a delightful forest and waterside walk run by the Forest Enterprise. Something to watch out for on the main road in Wootton is the **Minghella** ice cream factory, of particular interest to filmgoers and Italian ice cream lovers.

Little Canada Adventure Centre

New Road, Wootton

Action packed day for 8 – 16 year olds in a woodland setting. Activities include: quad-biking, abseiling, zip wire, karting, archery and circus skills, as well as ropewalks and adventure trails.

Advance booking is recommended.
For further information please call 3D on
☎ (01983) 885400.

Further south, **Parkhurst Forest** is a 1,100-acre (446 hectare), surprisingly unspoilt, tract of land, owned and run by the Forest Enterprise, which has a series of nature and forest trails for visitors. It is the only substantial piece of woodland on the Island and home to a large number of red squirrels. On the edges, but scarcely noticed by the walker, are the maximum security prisons – **Parkhurst** and **Albany** – and the short-stay **Camp Hill**. Parkhurst was originally a military hospital built in 1799, which opened as a prison and convict transportation depot in 1838 and was later extended. Albany was purpose built in 1963-6.

Coleman's Animal Farm

Coleman's Lane,
Near Porchfield
A hands-on experience with animals raised on the farm. Also wooden play area, large sandpit, and straw fun barn. Café & Gift Shop.
☎ (01983) 522831.
Open: 10am-5pm
Mid March-Oct.
Closed Mondays.
Admission charge.

OSBORNE HOUSE

Osborne House is a fascinating and revealing insight into the Victorian era and Royal family life, impressive both overall and in detail and attracting a great many visitors throughout the year. Osborne was built for Queen Victoria as a country retreat and family residence in 1845-8, 'a place of one's own, quiet and retired', away from the pressure of state ceremonial. It was her favourite residence after the death of Prince Albert in 1861 and where she herself died in 1901.

The present building was designed by Prince Albert, with the technical assistance of a leading London builder and entrepreneur, Thomas Cubitt. Osborne reflects the Prince's admiration for Italian art and architecture and the design is based on an Italian villa, with tall towers (campaniles) and a balcony (loggia). The flag tower is 107ft (33m) high and the clock tower 90ft (27m).

After Queen Victoria's death nobody in the Royal family was keen to live at Osborne, removed as it was from mainland society. Edward VII, who preferred Sandringham, gave Osborne to the nation as a memorial to his mother. The house opened to the public first in 1904 and its contents have remained substantially the same ever since. The State and private apartments used by Queen Victoria in the west and north wings are open to the public as are the gardens. The Royal Nursery suite has been open since 1989.

Immediately on arrival through the Prince of Wales' Gate, it is interesting to note that the site of the former Royal Naval College (1903-21), which was a preparatory establishment for Dartmouth, is now the main car park. It is recommended that a tour starts with the Royal apartments inside the house and continues outside afterwards. This may need to be adjusted depending on the weather or when the house is particularly busy.

Within the house itself, the tour takes in a succession of public and private rooms, lavishly furnished and decorated, which contain countless personal memorabilia and gifts from all over the world. The breathtaking **Durbar Room**, the expression of Victoria's status as Empress of India and constructed in 1893 to a design by an Indian architect, contains many reminders and artefacts from the sub-continent. There is an excellent illustrated souvenir guide produced by English Heritage. Visit arrangements in the house are seasonally adjusted: in winter visitors are taken on pre-booked guided tours by the custodians; in the busier summer months free flow access around the tour route applies.

Outside, on exiting from the Durbar wing, the upper terrace provides panoramic views and a pleasant stroll around the Royal Pavilion and Solent

Continued over page...

Continued from previous page...

frontage of the house. It also looks down on the lower terrace, with its Andromeda fountain and pergola, but this part of the garden is not open to the public. The newly restored walled garden opened in July 2000 and the design incorporates the initials V & A throughout. There are two original glasshouses with a wonderful array of colourful plants.

From the house, a path leads for half a mile (800m) to the **Swiss Cottage** and museum, which can also be reached by horse and trap (free with entry ticket). The Swiss Cottage is a very up-market Wendy House, in the style of a Swiss chalet, built in 1854. It was originally thought that it had been prefabricated abroad and put together at Osborne but restoration work in 1990 revealed that the estate carpenters actually built the structure.

Prince Albert intended the Swiss Cottage to be an educational device to teach his children the rudiments of housekeeping and cookery. A suite of functional rooms, including a pantry, kitchen, dining and sitting rooms, together with appropriate furnishings and utensils, helped the royal siblings get into the spirit of things. It was also a place where the children could house their growing collection of gifts, mementoes and natural history exhibits. These curious and personal items are now housed in a purpose built (1862) museum nearby.

Other items are worthy of notice in the gardens. Firstly, there is the ultimate boys' play area. The **Victoria Fort**, completed in 1856, after the Crimean war, is in miniature just like the Palmerstonian forts, which guard Portsmouth. The royal princes assisted with its construction and Prince Arthur helped add the **Albert Barracks** in 1860. Also, alongside the deckhouse of the Royal Yacht *Alberta* (1864) is **Queen Victoria's bathing machine**, with its changing room and WC.

Further Information

Facilities at Osborne include a reception area, toilets and two cafeterias ☎ (01983) 200022.
Open 10am-5pm daily from 1 April-30 Sept and 10am-4pm from 1-31 Oct. Phone for winter opening times, pre-booked tour details & entry prices. English Heritage members enter free.

NEWPORT

Newport is the capital and bustling administrative centre of the Island. Founded as a market town and port in the twelfth century, on the lowest fording point of the River Medina, it received its charter in 1180. It reached the height of its prosperity in the eighteenth-century, during the Napoleonic wars and still retains its commercial character today.

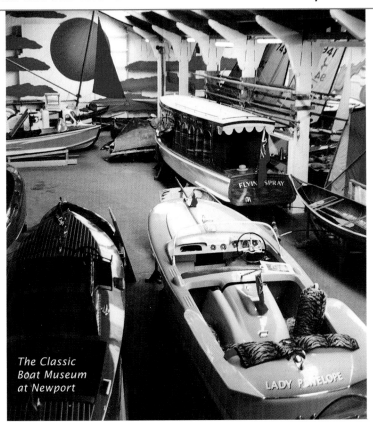

The Classic Boat Museum at Newport

Somehow Newport has just about kept its narrow streets, squares and a riverside. **St James Square** was the old market square until 1928 and is dominated by a memorial to Queen Victoria. The **High Street** contains some interesting (in passing) buildings, including the **Guildhall** (1814-16) by John Nash and the Castle Inn (1684). The shops have the familiar high street names, but many have hung on to their traditional character and building styles. Supermarkets and out of town developments have also proliferated in response to local and tourist demand.

St Thomas' Church was originally built in 1173 in what is now St James Square, but the church was demolished down to its window sills and

57

The Isle of Wight has a thriving ghost industry, based on centuries of tales and legends, some of them eminently plausible, and 'genuine' sightings. It all very much depends on what you believe. Over 200 sightings have been researched and catalogued by Gay Baldwin in her 4 popular books on Ghosts of the Isle of Wight.

Some of these lurid tales feature in the attraction, the Newport Ghost Walk, led by guides in period costume. The hour-and-a-half walk begins at the supposedly haunted Wheatsheaf Hotel in St Thomas's Square at 8pm every Wednesday night – from Easter to Halloween. Advance booking is recommended at any Isle of Wight TIC.

rebuilt in 1854 in the early Decorated style. Princess Elizabeth, the second daughter of Charles I who died in 1649, is buried in front of the altar. The memorial in Carrara marble was erected in 1856, as 'a token of respect for her virtues, and of sympathy for her misfortunes' by Queen Victoria. Other highlights include a carved oak pulpit and stone font, both from the 1630s, and a striking memorial to Sir Edward Horsey, Captain of the Island 1565-82.

Newport – Places to visit

The Museum of Island History
Newport Guildhall,
☎ (01983) 823366. Open: 10am-5pm Mon-Sat; 11am-3.30pm Sun

The Classic Boat Museum
The Quay, Newport Harbour
☎ (01983) 533493. Open April-Oct from 10.30am daily; restricted winter opening times.

Roman Villa
Cypress Road, Newport, Discovered in 1926 three rooms have well preserved mosaics and there is a diverse collection of domestic artefacts.
☎ (01983) 529720. Open: 10am-4.30pm Monday to Saturday, Easter to October. Admission charge.

The Quay Arts Centre
Sea Street, Newport, Former 18th century warehouses transformed into arts centre with café & bar. Varied programme of events. Open Mon to Sat. Call for details ☎ (01983) 822490.

IOW Bus & Coach Museum
The Quay, Newport, Isle of Wight Transport Heritage and memorabilia. Open on Sun, Tue, Wed & Thu from April-Sept and every day in August.
☎ (01983) 533352.

Farmer's Market – *every Friday in St Thomas' Square from 9am – 3pm.*

CARISBROOKE

Anglo-Saxon sources and scanty archaeological evidence suggest that Carisbrooke was the original capital of the Island in Jutish and Saxon times. Known as Wihtgarsburh, the town of Wihtgar, it probably gave its name at the time to the whole Island.

Medieval Knights at Carisbrooke Castle

During the medieval period, Carisbrooke, with its castle and Benedictine priory, was acknowledged to be the main market and administrative centre until the coastal and fishing trade of Newport grew substantially in the sixteenth century. The main attractions today are the castle and the church, although the village itself merits a brief stroll.

Carisbrooke Castle is well worth a detour on account of its imposing situation, lively history and substantial, interesting remains. The site was probably occupied in the late Roman period by a rectangular fort with bastions. What is certain is that the Normans built a castle during the tenure of William fitzOsbern as lord of the Island.

The castle still retains its classic motte-and-bailey shape, with a twelfth-century shell keep and curtain wall, but has had extensive *Continued on page 62...*

CHARLES I AND CARISBROOKE

S ome of the major events in the history of Carisbrooke Castle concern the stay and imprisonment on the Island of Charles I after his defeat in the First Civil War of 1642-5. During November 1647, when in negotiations with the Scots, Parliament and the Army about a settlement, Charles fled to the Isle of Wight, supposedly because of threats against his life by extremists in the New Model Army. He still had loyal supporters amongst the leading families of the Island, including the Oglanders and Worsleys and the Parliamentary Governor Colonel Robert Hammond was considered a moderate, with links to the Army Council.

On the King's arrival, Hammond, a 26-year old cousin of Oliver Cromwell, preserved the fiction that the King was a guest. In reality, Charles was closely watched while negotiations proceeded with the Scottish and English commissioners. However, he was allowed considerable freedom to move around the precincts of the castle, to go hunting and to visit local notables.

While stalling negotiations with the English commissioners, Charles had secretly concluded a deal with the Scots by which Parliament's erstwhile allies would invade England to coincide with a Royalist rising the following year. This would in effect mean a renewal of the Civil War. After rejecting all the English commissioners' proposals, Charles and his supporters decided that it was time for him to escape, but Hammond now dismissed the King's

Carisbrooke Castle

Apartments and museum, earthworks and masonry enclosures for children to explore and let off steam in the open. Large car park and good places for a picnic ☎ (01983) 522107.

Open: 10am-5pm April-Sept; 10am-4pm Oct-March.
English Heritage members free entry.

attendants and restricted his freedom further. The King walked under escort during the day and was locked in his chamber at night.

Royalist escape plots continued and eventually on 20 March 1648, Charles tried to escape through the first floor window of his lodging, but found that he had put on weight and the gap was not big enough. He was moved to another chamber and the ground beneath the window guarded by three soldiers. The gap in the window was enlarged by the removal of a bar with acid but another attempt on 28 May failed when the plot was betrayed.

During July and August 1648, the Second Civil War took place as had been planned at Carisbrooke the previous Christmas. The Army commanders, Fairfax and Cromwell, spent the summer and autumn defeating the Scots and suppressing the Royalist risings. Charles now attempted to come to terms with the Presbyterian (non-Army) members of Parliament, in the so-called Treaty of Newport, in the face of an aggrieved and increasingly radicalised Army, which, after a second civil war, was calling for the trial of the King as a 'man of blood'. Then, in a decisive coup ordered by Fairfax, Hammond was arrested on 27 November and taken to the Army Council. On 30 November, the King himself was arrested and taken to London for a trial, which ended with his execution on 30 January 1649.

thirteenth-century and later additions. The gatehouse is predominantly fourteenth-century and the internal buildings and artillery earthworks are from the Tudor period. Its attractive museum contains a collection of local archaeological and historic objects including personal relics of Charles I, transferred from Windsor Castle, and numerous paintings of local scenes and personalities.

Children are very likely to enjoy seeing the Well House, in which a trained donkey draws water on a tread-wheel from a well 161ft (49m) deep and sunk in 1130. The water depth varies between 15-70ft (5-21m) and every time the bucket is raised the donkey will have walked the equivalent of 422yd (386m).

St Mary's Church, of early Saxon foundation, was started in its present form by William fitzOsbern in 1070, and restored in 1907. In 1156, the site was given to the abbey of Lyre in Normandy and the French Benedictines built a priory, which incorporated the church. This priory thrived until it was dissolved by Henry V in 1414. It fell into ruin, but the church continued to serve the parish and its impressive tower was built in 1470. Look out for some notable memorials and graffiti from about 1440 outside the north wall of the church.

FURTHER SOUTH

Gatcombe is a remote, scattered hamlet, with a manor house, thatched cottages and an abandoned water mill, set amid lovely scenery. Its largely medieval church, St Olave's, has the oldest stained glass on the Island and an east window by Morris, Rossetti, Ford Maddox Brown and Burne-Jones. An early fourteenth-century wooden effigy of a crusading knight is associated with the odd disappearance, during a storm and eclipse in 1830, of an infatuated local girl called Lucy Lightfoot. The village itself allows easy access to tracks up onto the Downs.

Arreton is dominated by a handsome Jacobean manor house. The gardens and part of the house are currently open to the public during the summer. Tel (01983) 522604

The remarkably long village church, St George's, originating from Saxon

Arreton Old Village & Barns

The Dairyman's Daughter Pub and the Maltings Tearoom, Gift shop, Microbrewery, Woodcrafts, Lace, Lavender and Glassware. ☎ (01983) 528353

and Norman times and containing many noteworthy details, was restored in 1886 and is well worth the effort of a visit. Guided tours and trail Work Books are available.

The Island Brass-Rubbing Centre

Coach House behind Arreton Church
Practise brass-rubbing with wax on over fifty facsimiles of monumental brasses from all over the UK. Rubbings to take home. Shop for historical gifts and knick-knacks
☎ (01983) 527553.
Open: daily, except Sundays (by arrangement only), Easter to October.

The privately owned **Haseley Manor**, once a grange of the monks of Quarr, is one of the oldest manor houses on the Island.

Rookley and nearby **Chillerton** are set in attractive and varied walking country, Rookley used to be the centre of the Island's gravel quarrying and brickmaking industry. The modern Chequers Inn, through Rookley Green on the road to Niton, used to be a billet for Excise officers and is a free house. It has a large car park that can be used by walkers and, with food, amusements and an outdoor play area, is ideal for families.

Rookley Country Park

Off the Rookley to Shanklin road
22-acre (9-hectare) country park includes the Rookley Inn, which allows access to a fishing lake, a pitch and putt and a children's play area. Use of facilities for patrons only.
☎ (01983) 721606.

The 88-acre (36-hectare) **Robin Hill Country Park** is owned by the proprietors of Blackgang Chine and combines downland views, nature trails and picnic areas with over twenty theme park attractions such as a motion theatre, the Time Machine, a 440 yd (400m) toboggan run, and tree top adventure course. 'Colossus – the ultimate thrill' is the latest addition. There are also Roman villa excavations and woodland walks. It is mainly a summer attraction, but family events at weekends are organised in winter. Return visits are at discounted rates.

Robin Hill

Downend, nr Arreton
Open: 10am-5pm daily, April to October
☎ (01983) 730052.
www.robin-hill.com

Wightbyte

Old Gallows

Close to Robin Hill is the Hare and Hounds, the second oldest pub on the Island, from which hangings are reputed to have taken place on Arreton Down. One of those executed and displayed on the gibbet on Downend Gallows Hill was Micah or Michael Morey, a woodcutter, in 1735. He killed his grandson with an axe and tried to conceal the murder by burning down their shared cottage on top of the body. His ghost has been seen to walk on a number of occasions most recently 1974, in Burnt House Lane, around Robin Hill Country Park and near the Hare and Hounds.

The skull in the pub, which has been claimed as his, is older and may have come from a disturbed archaeological site on the Downs. One of the rafters is said to be the crossbeam of an old gallows. The local superstition held that a piece of wood from a gallows helped to ward off evil spirits.

Blackwater is a good starting point for walks over St George's Down on the eastern side of the Medina. The highest point is 363ft (111m) and there are fine views down the Medina Valley to the Solent and the mainland beyond. Carisbrooke can be seen clearly and the view stretches all the way round to St Catherine's and Shanklin Downs.

GODSHILL

Godshill is probably the best known and most photogenic village in the Island. It is uncompromisingly a tourist trap with its daily invasion of coach parties and numerous tea gardens and souvenir shops. For all that, it is a charming, thatched roofed village and is still well worth a visit, even out of season. It has a narrow, winding main street with tree-lined lanes and a church set delightfully on a hill, hence Godshill.

Legend has it that the villagers tried three times to build the church elsewhere, but every time found the stones removed to the current site. All Saints is in the top ten of UK churches which attract over 100,000 visitors a year. Yet another early medieval church belonging to the abbey of Lyre, it is notable for its unusual funerary monuments and a unique fifteenth century Lily Cross wall painting.

Further down, amid a host of tearooms and restaurants, the **Old Smithy** has a range of attractive shops (open all year) and gardens; its light meals and home-made cakes are excellent. Its garden attraction,

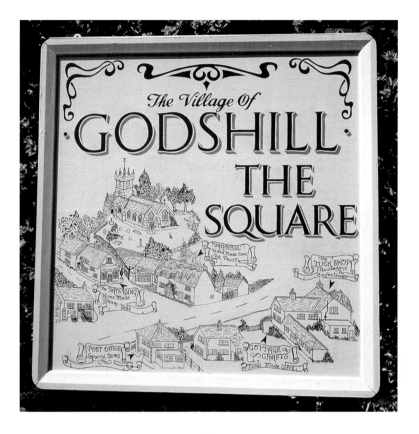

shaped like the Isle of Wight, incorporates models, grottoes, aviaries and the Godshill Witch.

A **Natural History Centre**, containing over 40,000 shells and displays of fossils, minerals and jewellery, opens daily from March to November ☎ (01983) 840333.

Godshill Model Village

Old Vicarage Gardens
Truly impressive 1:10 scale stone model village, with hundreds of dwarfed trees and 1:20 model railway
☎ (01983) 840270.
Open: 10.30am-4pm (5pm in April, May, June early July and September, dusk in late July and August except Saturday when it closes at 5.30pm), daily March to October.

Nostalgia Toy Museum

Godshill
Contains over 2,000 Dinky, Corgi and Matchbox toys dating from the 1930s to 1970s. Special annual and topical exhibitions, such as original Star Wars figures and Sindy dolls
☎ (01983) 840181.
Open: 10am-5pm Easter-October every day.

3. West Wight

Away from the bustle of the eastern coast, the western part of the Island, from St Catherine's Point to Alum Bay (known as the Back of Wight), is mostly a mixture of dramatic downland and precipitous sea-cliffs. The lower-lying land along the northern coast through Yarmouth and Newtown offers a gentler, varied, but equally impressive experience.

The downland hills and the rugged coast are full of unexpected delights and contrasts and the area has provided inspiration and relaxation for a host of literary figures. It is ideal for walks or a leisurely drive, with attractive, rolling countryside, peaceful villages and extensive views over land and sea.

The southern coast can be explored by bus, car and cycle along the Military Road (A3055) or on foot by the coastal path. This skirts the chines, as the steep, valley-like cracks leading to the sea are known,

eventually ending up at the spectacular chalk cliffs of Freshwater Bay, Alum Bay and the Needles. It gives memorable views of the sea along its entire length. The more energetic and adventurous can walk along the base of the crumbling cliffs near the water's edge.

Alternatively, a stroll or drive around the villages and Downs inland is just as rewarding, particularly as many of the Island's leisure trails intersect on the Downs. Car parks and short, circular walking routes along the coast and inland are plentiful.

YARMOUTH & THE NORTH COAST

Yarmouth is at least as old as the Domesday Book. It was given a charter in 1135 and was a medieval planned town, with its size restricted by its location on solid rock surrounded by the sea and the low-lying marshes of the estuary. As the nearest town of the Isle of Wight to the mainland, it used to export agricultural produce and livestock, while importing coal and manufactured goods. It was protected by a small, interesting castle built by Henry VIII, which was further strengthened under Elizabeth and in Stuart times. It is well preserved and has an informative and interesting exhibition.

Yarmouth Castle

English Heritage
☎ (01983) 760678.
Open 11am-4pm April to Sept.
Closed Friday & Saturday.

Yarmouth is the entry harbour for the ferries from Lymington and is a pleasant, old-fashioned port, which retains its distance. It tends to attract those 'yachties' who reject the hype of Cowes and the estuary is full of moorings and leisure craft, especially in summer.

Its shops, restaurants and pubs are inevitably geared towards the tourist and waterborne communities. That said, there is enough variety, quality and originality in the shops to interest and tempt browsers, typically in the Alchemist art gallery and bookshop in the High Street. Self-catering and waterborne visitors will be attracted by Angela's Delicatessen. Harwood's Chandlers and Ironmongers in particular will attract attention, even from land-lubbers.

In Norman times, the estuary at **Newtown** was much larger than it is today and was probably the best natural harbour on the Island. A thriving port and market town, Newtown (formerly Francheville) was the oldest borough (1256) on the Island (and until 1832 a 'rotten' one as well), but never recovered after a French raid of 1377 and the silting of the estuary. Only a cluster of farm buildings remains on the original site. The eighteenth-century **Town Hall** is a gem almost in the middle of nowhere; it has an interesting collection of borough documents and a replica of the town mace on view. Generally open some afternoons, April to October. Please check with custodian ☎ (01983) 531785.

Further inland and off the main road, the village of **Shalfleet** (meaning 'shallow creek') had, up until the seventeenth century, a quay which could take ships of up to 500 tons, carrying coal and other goods. With its inn, manor-house, water mill and thatched cottages it is worth a visit for its church alone. This is mainly late-thirteenth century, but with a Norman doorway and tower, originally designed as a tower of refuge, hence the 5ft (1.5m) thick walls and former lack of ground floor openings. Unfortunately, it had been built without foundations on 10ft (3m) of slipper clay and had to be underpinned in 1889 to prevent its collapse.

Walking routes

The broad Yar estuary has an undemanding, scenic 4-mile (6.4km) circular walk which would ease down a good lunch. It follows the western edge of the picturesque estuary, returning along the old railway line.

Just as it turns back to the north, a visit can be paid to All Saints at Freshwater and, if required, the Red Lion.

The Hamstead Trail runs for 7 miles (11.2km) from Yarmouth to **Brook** across the Downs to the south, starting at Hamstead Ledge (Details from Yarmouth TIC). The return can be co-ordinated with bus times.

To the east, the entire coast-line of the **Newtown** estuary and 4 miles (6.4km) of the adjacent coast [300 acres (122 hectares)] have been absorbed by the National Trust. The beautiful low-lying marshes of the estuary with 14 miles (23km) of creeks are largely unspoilt and sign-posted footpaths lead from Newtown to a Nature Reserve, one of the least frequented and peaceful parts of the Island. It is a particularly fruitful spot for birds (especially waders) and children and adults will enjoy exploring around the estuary on a dry day, possibly around the special 2-mile (3.2km) nature trail.

THE FRESHWATER PENINSULA

The Freshwater peninsula is all but cut off from the rest of the Island by the River Yar that flows north from its source near Freshwater Bay to the Solent at Yarmouth. This is West Wight proper whose seaside, dramatic scenery and countryside, as well as a wide range of shops and entertainment, make it a quiet, unhurried resort area, which rarely appears to be overwhelmed by crowds, even in high summer. It is ideal for a long weekend away from it all and there is something for everyone to enjoy.

Freshwater Bay

Arriving on the Peninsula from Yarmouth, the visitor will come immediately to **Fort Victoria Country Park** sited in another Victorian fort that commands fine views over the western Solent, close to the water's edge. It has free parking on the former parade ground, but is particularly crowded on yacht and power race days. Unless arriving on foot from Yarmouth (20 minutes) or by bus (only in summer), it is approached by a winding, narrow road, but there is ample parking.

The attractions are housed mainly in the arches of a 19th century brick battery. The Marine Aquarium contains a small collection of local fish and invertebrates, including the more unusual poisonous weevers and odd-shaped pipefish, and a tropical reef section. As well as a café, there is a small planetarium and a marine archaeology collection based around finds recovered locally.

A separate, modern building houses a large HO model railway, which claims to be the largest and most modern layout in the United Kingdom. At least twenty-five trains are running at any one time and visitors can operate some of the functions. It is obviously a must for railway enthusiasts and children will find it fascinating.

The seashore and woodland can also be explored along a nature trail (with way marks) or the coastal path. The stretch between the Fort and Yarmouth along the sea wall

Fort Victoria attractions

Marine Aquarium
Open Easter – October
☎ 01983-760283

Underwater Archaeology Centre
Open Easter – October
☎ 01983-761214

Model Railway
Open Easter- Sept
☎ 01983-761553

Island Planetarium@Fort Victoria
Please call for opening times
☎ 01983-761555

will take about 30 minutes, there and back. Overall, Fort Victoria is an adequate family attraction, especially on a rainy day, but the individual cost of each element will soon mount up. Just outside, on the approach road, is the more appealing Boathouse Café and Tearooms.

Hurst Castle, visible on a long spit of the mainland, which all but closes the western end of the Solent opposite, is one of a chain of so-called 'artillery' forts stretching from Cornwall to Kent. They were built by Henry VIII in the 1540s to protect the south coast against invasion by the French and Spanish. Other nearby forts on the mainland include those at Portland, Calshot and Southsea and, on the Isle of Wight, Yarmouth. Boat trips are available from Yarmouth.

Freshwater itself is a large, ill-defined sprawl that has grown around a scattering of hamlets, resorts and village greens. The church of All Saints, dating from the seventh century and incorporating Norman, other medieval and inevitably Victorian features, is well worth a detour. It has a great many interesting items and is notable as having been Tennyson's parish church. There are numerous memorials to the Tennyson family and Emily, Tennyson's wife, is buried in the churchyard. The Victorian stained glass is striking, especially the double window by G F Watts portraying Sir Galahad

Enjoy a ride on an open top bus, overlooking Alum Bay

which hides an interesting feature.

Totland Bay has a small, secluded and less frequented sand and shingle beach, suitable for fishing and bathing. Wide views of the Solent and Hurst Castle on the mainland can be obtained from the wooded cliffs above (along a path called the Turf Walk) or from the loftier Headon Hill, just to the south. **Colwell Bay**, immediately opposite Hurst Castle, has a long sandy beach (at low tide), rock pools and refreshments, which make it popular with families, and it does get crowded in high summer.

The Needles are three jagged chalk teeth marking the western extremity of the Island and are its best known landmark. A fourth 120ft (37m) steeple ('Lot's wife') collapsed in 1764 and the third rock is today the base for an automatic lighthouse, whose 1785-1859 predecessor used to stand on the mainland cliff above. Road services end nearby at Alum Bay and a half mile (0.8km) walk will be rewarded with one of the most distinctive views in Britain.

Boat trips to the Needles operate from Yarmouth, Alum Bay and Freshwater Bay. An exciting chairlift, or 181 steps, provides access to the beach at Alum and its twenty multi-coloured sands for which the place is famous. Also on site, Alum Bay Glass (open Easter to October) levies a small charge to watch glass being blown.

Radio transmission

In 1897, Marconi set up a 131ft (40m) high radio transmitter at the Needles Hotel with a receiver at Poole 18.6 miles (30km) away, to prove that his equipment could transmit across water and from shore to ship. A stone monument recalls the event.

A pleasant one mile (1.6km) walk (or Southern Vectis open-top bus every 30 minutes – 9.55am-5pm in summer and in good weather) will lead to **Needles Old Battery** (1862), a restored Victorian fort which has a 66yd (60m) tunnel, a welcome café and spectacular sea views.

The Needles Pleasure Park

Alum Bay
A loud, seemingly out-of-place gaggle of amusements including rides, an adventure playground and gift shops. All day parking charge. Free admission but rides and attractions have individual charges. On Thursday nights in August, a fireworks display takes place just after dusk. ☎ 0870 458 00 22. Open: 10am-5pm daily, Easter to October. Car parking charge. www.theneedles.co.uk

Needles Old Battery (NT)

Needles Headland
National Trust
☎ (01983) 754772.
Open: 10.30am-5pm, Sunday to Thursday, Easter to June and September and October; daily in July and August. Closes in bad weather, visitors should check by telephone on the day.

HMS Pomone

Wightbyte

In October 1811 the 38-gun frigate Pomone was returning from the Mediterranean when she struck a sunken rock just south west of the Needles Point. The crew were saved as were the guns and principal stores but not before some crew members had drunk themselves into a state of "extreme intoxication". The wreck of the ship was discovered about 10 years ago and has recently been excavated by marine archaeologists.

Tennyson

Alfred, Lord Tennyson, the son of a Lincolnshire rector, was born in 1809. He began writing poetry at the age of 8. In his early years, he wrote prolifically on classical myth and medieval legend, but was only financially secure in 1850, when he published *In Memoriam* and was appointed Poet Laureate. He married Emily Selwood in the same year. In the 1850s, he produced arguably his most famous poems, *The Charge of the Light Brigade*, *Maud* and *Idylls of the King* about the **Arthurian cycle**. Dying in 1892 and buried in Westminster Abbey, he is considered the most representative and popular poet of the Victorian era.

An Iona cross of Cornish granite stands high on the Downs. It is a memorial to Alfred, Lord Tennyson, raised in 1897, on one of Tennyson's favourite spots, although he was a habitual strider over all the Downs. The fine views from the memorial on Tennyson Down are worth the climb from Freshwater Bay, from Alum Bay or up a path from a car park just past the Highdown Inn at **Nodewell**.

Farringford House nearby was Tennyson's home from 1856 until 1867, when persistent crowds of admirers forced him to live at Aldworth, near Haslemere in Surrey, 'a haven of refuge against the invading Philistine'. Farringford is now a stylish, traditionally run hotel and its striking exterior can be seen along a tree-lined drive. The poem *Maud* mentions 'the house half-hid in the gleaming wood' and it actually paid for the house. Subsequent works enabled Tennyson to buy the land between Farringford and the sea, so that the view should not be spoiled.

Freshwater Bay has been formed by coastal erosion and the sand and shingle beach is only about 440yds (400m) wide. On sunny days, it does become crowded and the air can be bracing. There is a nearby 9-hole golf course at Afton Down for those who cannot lie on the beach all day. A curiosity, which may be viewed in passing, is St Agnes church. It was built of stone in 1908 with a thatched roof, about 33yds (300m) inland. For a breathtaking, circular ramble, easy access is available up on to Tennyson Down (3 miles/ 4.8km) and on to the Needles (5 miles/8km). Other walks can take in the variety of prehistoric remains on the Downs.

Dimbola Lodge was the nineteenth century home of Julia Margaret Cameron (1815-79), a pioneering Victorian photographer and friend of Tennyson, who established a literary and artistic salon around her in Freshwater Bay. It was a 'house indeed to which everyone resorted for pleasure and in which no man, woman or child was ever known to be unwelcome'.

Julia Margaret Cameron

Wightbyte

Julia was born in Calcutta in 1815. Educated in Europe, she returned to Calcutta where in 1838 she married Charles Hay Cameron, twenty years her senior. Ten years later the Camerons moved back to England where they became part of an artistic community based around Little Holland House in Kensington.

Julia visited Tennyson on the Isle of Wight and subsequently bought two cottages in Terrace Lane. They were linked by a central tower and renamed Dimbola Lodge after the Cameron family estates in Ceylon. A literary and artistic salon was established in Freshwater Bay. Julia built Tennyson a special gate so he could walk across the fields from Farringford in private.

In 1863, Julia was given a camera and she zealously photographed the great worthies of the day. She would also watch from her bedroom for willing victims and ambush them, much to their horror, as they walked by.

After being converted into holiday flats, the building was purchased in 1993 by the Julia Margaret Cameron Trust and now houses a permanent testament to Cameron's work as well as exhibitions of eminent photographers and photographic techniques. The museum is open all year round and there is an admission charge for the exhibition. For details 01983 756814 or www.dimbola.co.uk.

Nearby on the Newport Road garden lovers will enjoy a visit to Afton Park Gardens open every day in season. The seven acre site has something for everyone: a summer garden, an apple walk, plant nursery, wildflower meadow, orchard and Café. www.aftonpark.co.uk or 01983 755744

BACK OF WIGHT –
COMPTON TO NITON

This coast between the Needles and Compton, with its towering chalk cliffs has probably the most spectacular scenery on the Island, much of it owned by the National Trust. Along the shore, there are numerous arches, stacks and caves, which can best be examined from seaward. Compton Bay has a fine sandy beach, which is good for bathing and suitable for surfing.

Isle of Wight Pearl is a jewellery manufacturing and outlet centre, specialising in cultured and simulated pearls (pearl-based jewellery can be purchased, from £9-£16,000). Smaller retail units cater for silver, crystal, gold and diamonds. ☎ (01983) 740352.

Close to Brighstone on the Military Road, the **Dinosaur Farm Museum** is sited on farmland owned by the Jones and Philipps families. Owing to coastal erosion, the farm is losing 1 metre a year, resulting in the gradual exposure of fossils and dinosaur bones. In 1992, the curator of the IOW Geology Museum at Sandown was searching for fossil remains and found a large rib, which led to the discovery of a spectacular brachiosaurus skeleton. Although not complete, it is one of the most impressive finds of its kind in Europe.

As the IOW Geology Museum Field Centre, it contains not only the brachiosaurus remains, but also a variety of exhibits from the museum at Sandown. Dinosaur bones are preserved and catalogued in the old milking shed and hay loft. The processes and exhibits are fascinating and the hands-on approach, with a dinosaur themed play area and fossil workshop, particularly appeals to children.

Dinosaur Farm Museum

A3055 near Brighstone
Enthusiastic and successful fossil hunts three or four times a week in summer; they depend on the tide and must be booked in person and paid for in advance ☎ (01983) 740844. www.dinosaur-farm.co.uk Open: Open most days April-Oct. Please call to check opening times.

The area between the Downs and the sea combines sandy ridges and clay levels. Formerly, settlements lay along a track at the foot of the Downs leaving the coast remote and exposed. A 10-mile (16km) stretch of coastal road, **the Military Road**, was built in the 1860s to improve defence arrangements in the event of (French) invasion and allow more rapid communications with West Wight, but was not metalled until the 1930s.

Coastal erosion has brought the road steadily closer to the sea, for safety's sake, movement has to be measured by tiltmeters. This southwest coast has been eroded at the rate of 11.5ft (3.5m) a year, although some occasions have seen losses of 98-295ft (30-90m) after heavy rainfall. Numerous paths allow access to the sea-cliffs and lanes lead inland to the Downs and villages.

The Military Road leads eastwards to **Chale**. The church, St Andrew's, is exposed to the same weather, which has, together with the nearby **Atherfield Ledge** in **Chale Bay**, filled so much of the churchyard. The memorials and graves of seafarers who perished on the treacherous coast nearby can be seen clustered around a twelfth-century church, painted by William Turner in his early years. Well frequented and used for storage when Chale was the smuggling capital of the Island, it has had progressive updates throughout the medieval period and in the nineteenth century.

The coast at this point is dominated by **Blackgang Chine**, plausibly named after a smuggling band active in the eighteenth-century, but more likely deriving from the black clay cliffs and the word *gange* meaning a pathway. The chine is a good deal shorter than the forbidding and deep 4,592ft, (400m) long ravine it once was at the start of the nineteenth century.

Compton Bay view

Smuggling

The Island has long been associated with smuggling because of the remoteness of its southern coast and its general proximity to the mainland. The eighteenth-century saw the heyday of smuggling in reaction to systematic enforcement of Excise Duty on a range of imported goods, notably tobacco and spirits (nothing changes!). Enormous black economy profits were to be made and the chines allowed easy, hidden access to the beach while vessels offloading were able to conceal themselves under the cliffs.

The problem was so great that in the eighteenth-century eleven excise officers guarded the 17 miles (27km) between Ventnor and Freshwater. By 1836, sixteen coastguard stations along the Wight's south coast, numerous revenue cutters and two wherries offshore had just about managed to control the situation. Punishment was draconian by today's standards – imprisonment, transportation or years of service in the Navy.

Starting in 1842, Alexander Dabell built a scenic garden in and above Blackgang Chine to attract the growing numbers of Victorian tourists. Further extensions of the gardens and a range of entertainments have been forced to adapt to cope with the remorseless advance of the sea and the effects of erosion in a process of what is known as managed retreat. Indeed, in 1994, a third of the park was displaced.

Progressively, from the 1970s, the site, still owned and run by the Dabell family, has developed a 40-acre cliff top site containing a multi-layered and multi-themed park which will delight children. Children can play on many features including the Water Force ride, with rubber boats rushing down 100m runs, enjoy animated indoor shows and themed activity areas.

Parents will have to content themselves with gardens, St Catherine's Quay – Maritime World and Blackgang Sawmill – World of Timber. The park attempts to provide a balance of educational adventure and fun, but to be fair the fun and commercialisation rather pre-dominate. In busy months, especially at weekends, the place is packed out and full of opportunities to spend money.

Blackgang Chine

A3055 west of Ventnor
☎ 01983 730052. Open: 10am-5.30pm daily, Easter to October. Floodlit evenings in high season.
www.blackgangchime.com

Close by, commanding views above the 500ft cliffs and from a nature trail of 2.5 miles (4km) are worth the effort. Access to both starts from the View Point car park.

Far above and out of sight, on the second highest point on the Island,

is **St Catherine's Oratory**. It was built in 1314 as penance by the local landowner for an appropriated cargo of French wine. Until the 1530s, a chantry priest maintained the light and prayed for those lost at sea. From a car park on the coast road below, a brisk climb up a well-worn footpath will be rewarded with outstanding views all round (1 hour up and down).

The **Hoy Monument**, commemorating a visit by Tsar Alexander I in 1823 and later adapted as a Crimea war memorial, is visible high inland. Provision for a picnic would add to the pleasure, as even during the height of the summer season, the climb, which is not excessive, deters the casual visitor.

Niton is an unremarkable residential village, but is a good starting point for rambles. Its church, dating from Norman times, has table-top tombs, used extensively in the past for smuggling and hiding fugitives, and the graves of the St Catherine's lighthouse staff killed during a German bombing raid in 1943.

St Catherine's Lighthouse

Nr Niton
10-minute walk down to the lighthouse from the road. Open: normally 1-5pm from Tuesday to Fridays, at Easter and Whitsun and from mid-June until the end of September.

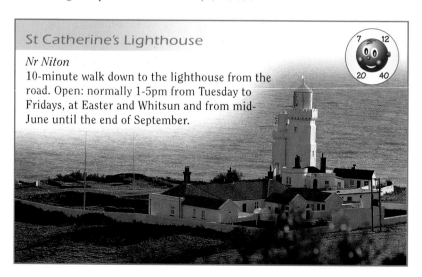

The southernmost tip of the Island is **St Catherine's Point**, occupied by the twin-towered lighthouse, built in 1837-40 and known locally as the 'cow and calf' (the smaller tower housed a now discontinued fog signal). The light is automatic, but former keepers give a stimulating 20-minute tour of the Victorian lighthouse, which includes a climb to the top of the 89ft (27m) structure and a view of its formidable lamp. Children will enjoy the climb and the unfamiliar features; adults the unusual theme and the stunning sea view.

Wrecks and lifeboats

Wightbyte

St Catherine's and Chale Bay have the highest number of recorded wrecks on the Island - fourteen in one night in 1757. Between 1830 and 1900 more than 270 ships were wrecked along the coast, mostly sailing vessels unable to cope with the strong Atlantic south-westerlies and the peculiar properties of the tidal streams around the Island. One of the most notorious, the *Clarendon* in 1836 and its widely reported total loss of life (mostly women and children), led directly to the building of the St Catherine's Point lighthouse.

From the 1860s, volunteer local men crewed the lifeboats (under sail and oars), established from Brighstone and Brook, which rescued the more fortunate. The records of their considerable achievements can be seen in local churches, most typically at Brighstone. Jack Seely, the 1st Lord Mottistone, served as crew, coxswain and supporter for forty years.

INLAND

The broad expanse of rolling downland set back from a coast that is nearly always in view, is part of the east-west spine of the Island. It is highly popular with walkers and cyclists, but never seems crowded. It can be enjoyed along several long distance paths or on shorter circular routes. The villages are easily accessible by car.

The centre of **Brighstone** is one of the Island's most picturesque villages. It is a first-class place to start a ramble or walk: there is a nature trail in Brighstone Forest and many trails on the Downs can be accessed.

Its church has an abundance of medieval and later features and a memorial to a Victoria Cross recipient in the churchyard. A glance at the memorial boards to the Brighstone lifeboat reveals that 433 lives were saved over fifty-five Victorian and Edwardian years. Opposite, there is a tiny but worthwhile museum, which has mementoes of village life, in an attractive terrace of thatched cottages in North Street next to a National Trust shop.

Towards the coast, Grange and Chilton Chines can be reached by paths from the coast road and bathing at high tide in the area is quiet and enjoyable away from the crowds.

Shorwell is a pretty, neat village that mixes stone cottages with thatched roofs and modern buildings sympathetically. Its church and pub make it well worth a visit, particularly around lunch-time. St Peter's church is full of interesting features with an especially well-written guide available on site. Family memorials, a fifteenth-century wall painting and a blocked arch through which the village's defensive cannon was wheeled out are just a few of the many details.

Recommended walks from Brighstone

Brighstone Forest, 2.5-mile (4km) trail. Car park on the Brighstone-Calbourne road.

Worsley Trail – This trail runs 15 miles (24km) from Brighstone to Shanklin.

Tennyson Trail – This runs from Carisbrooke to Alum Bay, but Brighstone is a good place to intercept the trail and head west, to pick up views and Tennyson reminders, either returning along the same route or along the coast. The round trip is about 12 miles (19km).

Three large manor houses – North Court, West Court and Wolverton Manor – whose former residents are well represented on memorials in the church and churchyard – are in or around the village.

Mottistone is grouped around a delightful manor house, which has successively been the home of the Cheke, Dillington and Seely families. After a landslip in 1706, it became a farmhouse until bought as part of the estate in 1861 by Charles Seely of Brook House. His grandson, General Jack Seely, later 1st Baron Mottistone, organised the removal of 1,400 tons of soil from the buried east wing, before moving into Mottistone, and, by the time of his death in 1947, had restored the manor house. His son, John Seely, an architect of distinction, had assisted in the restoration and bequeathed the estate to the National Trust in 1963.

The church dates from the twelfth-century, with heavy alterations in the fifteenth and nineteenth-centuries. Despite this, it has retained its medieval character and is worth a stop to look at the memorials and tombs. The chancel roof is made from cedar planks from the wreck off Brighstone of the barque *Cedrene* in 1862 . Near Mottistone, on the hill above, is the **Longstone**, the remains of a Neolithic long barrow, which can be reached after a short climb along a path from the manor house.

Brook is a quiet, unassuming and widespread village which takes its name from the stream that flows through it. The medieval church on its mound, St Mary the Virgin, was rebuilt after a fire of 1862 and retains very few original features. It contains a board recording the exploits of the *George and Annie, William Slaney Lewis and Susan*

Mottistone Manor Garden (NT)

☎ (01983) 741302

Open: Open 11am-5.30pm April-October. Closed Fri & Sat.

Ashley, lifeboats of Brook. South of the Military Road, at Brook Chine, there is a secluded beach near Hanover Point off which the fossilised stumps of a former pine forest, known as the 'pine raft', can be seen, covered in seaweed. J B Priestley lived for a time in Brook Hill House.

Just to the north at Shalcombe is Chessell Pottery-Café centred in a large converted barn. For many years the distinctive Chessell pottery was produced here but the business has recently changed hands. You can now decorate your own pottery in a working studio.

The ancient manor of **Calbourne** is a cluster of thatched cottages, set amid fields and woods. The highlight is **Winkle Street**, a highly photogenic row of stone and thatched cottages opposite the River Caul.

In the vicinity are two large houses: Westover, a large eighteenth-century building, and Swainston Manor, now a hotel and restaurant, dating from Norman times and once owned by the bishops of Winchester. Swainston, an important estate held by many illustrious medieval families and the Crown, was substantially rebuilt in 1750, but retained many original features, notably the twelfth-century hall and bishop's chapel. It was completely gutted by a German incendiary bomb in 1941, but has been carefully restored.

Despite its Saxon origins, Calbourne church today dates from the thirteenth-century, when the estate belonged to the Bishops of Winchester, and has memorials up to the present day. To the west of the village, there is the seventeenth-century working **Calbourne Water Mill** with a collection of historic farm implements, set in a rural location. It is a convenient and restful place to stop for coffee and tea. Seasonal opening ☎ (01983) 531227.

Chessell Pottery-Café

Decorating studio, gift shop and café.
☎ (01983) 531248
www.pottery-café.com
Open daily all year round.

BY THE WAY

If you have time on your hands before or after the crossing between the mainland and the Isle of Wight, you might wish to consider what is available in the main Hampshire ports that connect with the Island.

PORTSMOUTH

The country's premier naval base with many daily shipping movements which are listed in the Portsmouth News and on its associated website. To see the ships at close quarters the best vantage point is the Round Tower at the harbour entrance. For a bird's eye view of the harbour and surrounding area try the 170m high Spinnaker Tower opened in 2005. It is located in Gunwharf Quays, a designer outlet complex with a variety of restaurants, cafés and bars on the waterfront close to the Wightlink car ferry terminal and the foot passenger service to Ryde.

In the Dockyard:

- *HMS Victory* – Nelson's flagship at Trafalgar, preserved in dry dock. Guided tours within the ship reveal the layout and equipment of a heart-of-oak man-of-war of the eighteenth-century.

- *HMS Warrior* 1860 – berthed near the entrance. Britain's first ironclad, painstakingly restored to her pristine condition.

- *Mary Rose* – raised from the sea off Southsea castle in 1982, the most complete Tudor warship to have survived. Dedicated museum of recovered artefacts.

- *Royal Naval Museum* – with the Trafalgar Experience – walk-through account of the battle of Trafalgar.

- *Action Stations* – an interactive attraction showing the Royal Navy in action.

Nearby Old Portsmouth:

- Harbour fortifications including the fifteenth century Round Tower, the Square Tower and several eighteenth and nineteenth-century gun batteries.

- Domus Dei medieval church.

- Anglican Cathedral of St Thomas a Becket.

- Amusement arcades and fairground at Funacres.

Southsea Seafront:

- 3-mile (4.8km) long, partly backed by the Common, a large stretch of recreational grass.

- Blue Reef Aquarium.

- D-Day Museum.
- Royal Marines Museum.
- Southsea Castle (Henry VIII coastal fort).
- The Pyramids (an indoor leisure pool and water attraction).

SOUTHAMPTON

- Stroll along medieval town walls with numerous towers.
- Bargate – Norman gateway.
- Medieval Merchant's House in French Street.
- Maritime Museum in the old Wool House.
- God's House Tower, the city's Archaeological Museum.
- Medieval merchant's hall.
- The Tudor House Museum in Bugle Street.
- A *Titanic* trail, circuit of places associated with the famous White Star liner.
- West Quay Shopping Centre
- *Mayflower* memorial, which is virtually opposite the Royal Pier.

LYMINGTON

- Charming New Forest town, the port for the ferry traffic to Yarmouth and home to a great many yachts and leisure craft.
- Quay Hill has a particularly tempting selection of small shops.
- St John the Baptist's Church has a memorial to those lost in 1941 in the sinking of *HMS Hood* by the German battleship *Bismarck*.

Near Lymington:

- Spinners, a garden which is open April-September, has a dazzling display of magnolias, azaleas, hydrangeas and rhododendrons on wooded slopes leading down to the Lymington River.
- Exbury Gardens, owned by the Rothschilds, on the Beaulieu River, which has a particularly stunning array of shrubs and flowers.
- Bucklers Hard with its Maritime Museum and planned model village.
- Beaulieu, home to the famous National Motor Museum, the nine-teenth-century Palace House and the ruins of Beaulieu Abbey itself.
- The more adventurous might wish to try an excursion into the New Forest, but it is worth remembering that, especially en route to the Isle of Wight, time and tide…

The Isle of Wight is a very flexible tourist facility and an ideal location for those based on the South Coast to enjoy a day trip or short break. Equally, there is a wealth of things to do during a longer holiday on the Island. It is an opportunity just simply to relax by walking the wonderful footpaths or by sitting in a deckchair on the beach. Many families repeatedly return to the Island and enjoy all the facilities that it has to offer. Even if the weather is inclement, there are plenty of options to keep both adults and children amused.

If you are spending a short time on the Island, planning makes it more worthwhile. In almost every case, a good map of the Island is essential, either from the Ordnance Survey series or the cheerful A-Z Isle of Wight Visitors' map. Attraction opening times should be checked.

MOTORING

It is easy to take a car to the Island, which has nearly 500 miles (805km) of good quality roads and direction signs, although motorists may wish to look at the off-peak pricing arrangements available from the ferry operators for crossing the Solent. As a matter of fact, mile for mile, it is the most expensive crossing in the world.

Once on the Island, the motorist will find that away from the prime tourist spots and town centres, the Island is relatively free of congestion. Newport, Ryde, Sandown and Shanklin can at times be very busy, but, generally, the Island is well served with traffic schemes and car parks. Access is provided along metalled roads to all but the most remote visitor sites and most attractions have adequate parking. Motorists will want to note that petrol is usually one or two pence per litre more expensive on the Island. The many narrow and winding country roads on the Island will inhibit speed and the only stretch of dual carriageway (1.5 miles) is in Newport.

Out of season, most of the more popular attractions can be sighted in a single day, although time spent actually visiting them might also be required. One day will allow a pleasant, leisurely drive around the whole coast of the Island, with regular stops for refreshment. In season, more time will be required and the day motorist will probably wish to choose highlights or themes that he or she wishes to pursue. Suggestions for these are given later.

BEACHES

The Isle of Wight has a great many beaches, most of which are suitable for bathing. Care should be exercised with regard to the prevailing wind and sea conditions, as well as the state of the tide. In terms of cleanliness, facilities and amenities, the Island's beaches continue to be nominated for and to win awards for excellence.

Ryde

Has three wide, sandy beaches: **Ryde West Sands**, **Ryde East Sands** and **Puckpool**. Safe, shallow bathing with adult and children's facilities adjacent to the beach. Good for sandcastle building and has a seawater tidepool, but watch out for that tide coming in.

Seaview

A well known spot for sailors – three beaches: **Springvale**, **Seagrove Bay** and **Priory Bay**. Rock pools.

St Helen's Bay

This is good for swimming and has rock pools and a sandy beach. Behind the Duver are sand dunes, which are the habitat for lots of wildlife.

Sandown

With its long sandy beach and developed facilities, Sandown is the ideal family beach, for both sand and swimming. It can get crowded though.

Shanklin

Three adjoining beaches: **Hope**, **Esplanade** and **Appley** provide a good, sandy shoreline in the shelter of steep cliffs. Access to beach is by road, foot or from the upper town via the lift. Good swimming and excellent sandcastle terrain.

Lifeguard patrols are a feature of three Isle of Wight beaches: Ryde, Sandown and Shanklin during the summer months May – Sept from 10am-6pm. These three beaches have been designated European Blue Flag Beaches.

Continued over page...

The Beach at Shanklin

Continued...

Bonchurch

A quiet sandy beach with rockpools at low tide

Ventnor

This sand/shingle beach shelves steeply and has strong waves, next to a small esplanade. Bathing is safe, with opportunities for boating and angling.

Compton Bay

One of the most popular beaches on the Island, a mile (1.6km) long stretch of sand, good for swimming and walking. It can be windy and is consequently frequented by windsurfers and surfers. At low tide, pools of water are left behind, making it popular with small children. Older children may enjoy looking for fossil and dinosaur bones.

Freshwater Bay

An attractive, sheltered bay with limited sand and pebbles. The beach shelves deeply into the sea, so swimmers should take great care.

Alum Bay

Famous for its multi-coloured sands and scenery, the beach is pebbly. Strong tidal currents mean caution should be exercised. Access is by chair lift or on foot from the Needles Pleasure Park.

Totland Bay

A pleasant family resort and popular beach with safe swimming, the bay is sheltered and the beach combines sand and shingle.

Colwell Bay

A busy family resort with a long beach. At low tide a good stretch of sand is revealed, ideal for paddling, swimming and building sandcastles.

Gurnard Bay

Good for family bathing, with a gently shelving sand and shingle beach. Surfing and sailing are possible and there are limited facilities.

West Cowes

The sand and shingle beach makes an interesting viewing point for watching sailing in the Solent.

East Cowes

A good vantage point for watching the yacht racing. A children's paddling pool and playground are next to the beach.

Bembridge

Another well known sailing centre which has a foreshore on three sides. Beach and rock pools tend to disappear at high tide so timing is vital.

Whitecliff Bay

Steep cliff access, but along a picturesque path. The sandy beach is safe for swimming, and there is a café.

Relaxing at Alum Bay

OUT & ABOUT
ON PUBLIC TRANSPORT

Sightseeing bus trip

Buses

Southern Vectis is the only company that runs an extensive network of public bus services on the Isle of Wight. The company produces a comprehensive bus timetable twice a year for a minimal cost. Summer and winter timetables are available from Isle of Wight Tourism. A variety of Rover tickets are offered for individuals and families, valid for one, two, seven or twenty-eight days' unlimited travel. This also includes travel on Island Line trains but is not valid on 'Nightclubber' services. The Rover ticket also entitles allows discounts on certain admission prices. For further information ☎ (01983) 532373 or www.southernvectis.com.

The main tourist bus service is the 7 or 7A which, during the season, provides an hourly bus around the Island in both directions, allowing visitors to leave and join the bus as many times as they like. These buses have a unique blue livery. Various other coach companies offer excur-

sions around the Island and the local press should be checked for details. A free bus, 'the Wight Delight' operates between Brickfields Horsecountry, Waltzing Waters and Flamingo Park.

Trains

The Island Line runs from Ryde Pierhead to Shanklin. It has intermediate stations at Ryde Esplanade, St John's, Smallbrook Junction, Brading, Sandown and Lake. There are normally two trains an hour, with Rover and discount tickets available. The trains synchronise with Ryde Pierhead Catamaran arrivals. Ryde Esplanade Station ☎ (01983) 562492. www.island-line.co.uk

Cycling

Cycling on the Island is strongly supported by the Island Council. The cyclist has a vast network of country roads, bridle paths and rugged terrain to enjoy. Old railway lines and cycleways allow easy access to traffic-free areas and details of routes can be obtained from the Island Tourist Information Centres.

For off road enthusiasts, the Isle of Wight Council has published an attractive booklet which details mountain biking routes on the Island. They range from gentle leisure rides to day long rides for the hardened enthusiast.

Further details in the Fact File.

WALKING

The Island has over 500 miles (805km) of paths in an area of only 127 useable square miles (38,000 hectares). The Coastal Path can be walked in four days at a reasonable pace and is a series of constantly changing and contrasting views. Nearly half is preserved 'Heritage Coast' and its best bits are administered by the National Trust (a useful, personal website is www.mortiboy.com). Inland, there are walks over downland, through unspoilt country villages and through woods and fields, which include some well signposted and maintained longer distance trails.

Walking on the Tennyson Trail

A Coastal Paths booklet is available from tourist offices and includes:South-East: Bembridge to Niton; South-West: Niton to Alum Bay; North-West: Alum Bay to Cowes; North-East: Cowes to Bembridge. Numerous books and leaflets are available which detail walks suited to individual temperament and capability.

Themed walking trails

These are suitable all year except in extreme conditions.

- The Bembridge Trail runs from Newport to Bembridge windmill through the southern part of the chalk downs, with some woods and good all round views. 15 miles (24km).

- The Hamstead Trail from Yarmouth to Brook passes though Newtown, agricultural land and the Downs. 8 miles (13km).

- The Nunwell Trail runs between Ryde and Lake Common across water meadows, downs and agricultural land. 10 miles (16km).

- The Shepherd's Trail from Whitcombe Cross, near Carisbrooke, to Atherfield along mainly high downland with extended views. 10 miles (16km).

- The Stenbury Trail is between Blackwater (Newport) and Ventnor, passing through downlands and shallow valleys. 10 miles (16km).

- The Tennyson Trail runs from Carisbrooke to Alum Bay, taking in downland, forest and views of the sea, and is probably the most exhilarating walk on the Island. 15 miles (24km).

- The Worsley Trail goes from Brighstone to Shanklin along the southern part of the Island, with some forest and high-level walking. 15 miles (24km).

- A modestly priced booklet entitled "Coastal Paths and Inland Trails" is produced by Isle of Wight Tourism and gives detailed directions and information on these trails. They are available at all IOW Tourist Information Centres.

THEMES

The use of themes produces an ideal framework for exploring the Island in detail, either on foot, by cycle or by less energetic forms of transport, especially for those who like to learn something while they are travelling or for those whose leisure needs to have some purpose or pattern. A few areas are suggested which may stimulate and appeal to the visitor.

Second-hand Bookshops

There are several second-hand and antiquarian bookshops on the Island, which will appeal to the general browser and specialist collector. They have a regular turnover of books, the prices are competitive in almost every case and the stock will appeal to a wide variety of tastes. Charity shops and other secondhand/antique/bric-a-brac outlets also stock an indiscriminate selection of titles, which are worth a browse, particularly in Newport and Ryde. Book fairs take place periodically, details of which can be obtained from any of the bookshops.

Literary Associations

The Isle of Wight is a fertile ground for tracing resident and transient authors and poets, as well as their associations with the Island:

Matthew Arnold, W H Auden, Jane Austen, Lewis Carroll, Charles Dickens, Henry Fielding, Celia Fiennes, Thomas Hardy, Christopher Isherwood, Henry James, Frances Kilvert, Edward Lear, Henry Longfellow, John Keats, Rudyard Kipling, Thomas Nashe, Alfred Noyes, J B Priestley, Alfred Lord Tennyson, Aubrey de Selincourt, Algernon Swinburne, H de Vere Stacpoole to name but a few.

Manor Houses

The Island's wealth of manor houses, principally Elizabethan and Jacobean, are dotted all over the Island, but mostly in the inland south and east. Many serve as hotels, private residences and farmhouses, but some have access for the public. All have been mentioned in the text of this book but the best book devoted to the subject is *The Manor Houses of the Isle of Wight* by C W R Winter (Published in 1984, it is now out of print).

Churches

Churches on the Island represent good way points for those who wish to have a theme or purpose when they travel. Virtually every village has a historic church of some sort, generally dating from Norman times, although many are not particularly memorable from an architectural point of view. What they do have are a great many oddities, unusual memorials and curious features which crop up as surprises in practically every case and each one seems to have a story to tell. Most have been built with local stone, either limestone or Upper Greensand free-stone except for some traces of Caen stone and Purbeck marble.

It will be clear that many of the parishes, particularly in the south and west of the Island, have thriving and enthusiastic communities, which take good care of their churches. They are generally open during daylight hours or the key is available from a willing neighbour.

The visitor will decide from the text those churches, which he or she wants to see, and may want to visit according to theme, geographic area or historic period. Certainly, those of Norman foundation, which include the majority, naturally group together, while the Victorian taste can be indulged in the resort towns of the South-East, at Whippingham and in Ryde. The churches that should not be missed are those at: Arreton, Brading, Brighstone, Calbourne, Carisbrooke, Godshill, All Saints, Ryde, Shorwell and Whippingham.

Gardens

The Isle of Wight is known as the 'Garden Isle' because of its rich variety of different natural habitats and environments concentrated in a small area, caused by subtle climate variations, the sea air and the wide geological diversity. Thus, contrasting characteristics exist within a few miles of each other, such as the pseudo-tropical conditions of Ventnor and the Undercliff, the rugged salt laden south-west coast and the open chalk downlands. This diversity is reflected in the range of gardens on the Island.

Appuldurcombe House gardens were laid out at the end of the eighteenth century by Capability Brown. Skilful planting, serpentine drives,

'eye-catchers' and viewpoints on top of the surrounding downs created an illusion of size. Much of this is no longer visible but work is being carried out by English Heritage to restore the immediate park surroundings to their early nineteenth-century grandeur. There are currently 11 acres (4.5 hectares) of grounds surrounding the house.

Morton Manor Garden near Brading is immaculately cultivated by the Trzebski family. Spring blooms are followed by rhododendrons, azaleas, camelias and magnolias. As well as the traditional herbaceous borders, there are a formal Rose Garden and an Elizabethan Sunken Garden, which has enviable box hedges.

Mottistone Manor Garden is modern in comparison with the age of the adjacent fifteenth and sixteenth-century manor house. There are three parallel gardens, approached by a flight of steps from the entrance courtyard: the rose garden, fruit trees under-planted in summer with vegetables, and the main walk, which passes between a pair of long colourful herbaceous borders. Higher up, grassy terraces are planted with differing pairs of fruit trees – quinces, plums, gages, apples and sweet cherries.

Nunwell House has 5 acres (2 hectares) of beautifully set formal and shrub gardens. A great avenue of lime trees leads up to the front of the eighteenth-century house. The gardens were replanted in the early 1960s and the current owners continue to refurbish them.

Osborne House Gardens. 50 acres (20 hectares) are open to the public including the formal Italian garden and terraces to the rear of the house. Sweeping parkland leads down to

Swiss Cottage with the charming cottage gardens. Lebanon cedars, magnolias, rhododendrons and azaleas line the pathways around the estate and there is a delightful walled kitchen garden. Specialised garden tours occur in the summer.

Ventnor Botanic Gardens features a wide variety of species. It comprises cliff top grassland and sea cliffs to the south and a cliff face to the north. A walk around the gardens takes in the Mediterranean Terrace, the Rock & Scree Bank, the Victorian Sub-Tropical Palm Garden, the Medicinal Garden, the New Zealand Garden, the Hydrangea Dell, the Japanese Garden and the Americas Collection. The refurbished Temperate House displays mostly southern hemisphere plants. Open daily from March – October. Restricted opening in winter months. Visitor centre, shop, café and plant sales www.botanic.co.uk (01983) 855397.

National Gardens Scheme

Every year, private gardens open to the public on specific days under the National Gardens Scheme. This is a rare opportunity to see private gardens in beautiful settings in support of a variety of charities. Specific details can be obtained from the current leaflet at the Tourist Office or local Island library.

Ventnor Botanic Gardens

Suggested Themed Day Itineraries

Animals

- Brickfields – Butterfly World.
- Flamingo Park at Seaview – Sandown Zoo.
- Isle of Wight Donkey Sanctuary – Isle of Wight Owl & Falconry Centre at Appuldurcombe.

Food and Drink

- Rosemary Vineyard – Morton Manor Vineyard – Adgestone Vineyard – Lunch in Ryde, St Helen's or Seaview.

Gardens

- Morton Manor – Shanklin Chine – Ventnor Botanic Gardens .
- Appuldurcombe -Ventnor Botanic Gardens – Mottistone Manor Gardens (when open).

Heritage and History

- Yarmouth Castle – Newtown Old Town Hall – Newport Roman Villa.
- Carisbrooke Castle – Osborne House.
- St Catherine's Lighthouse – Brighstone Village Museum – Needles Old Battery.
- Brading Roman Villa – Bembridge Windmill – Nunwell House.

Railways

- Model Railway, Fort Victoria – Isle of Wight Model Railways Exhibition and Museum, Cowes – Isle of Wight Steam Railway at Havenstreet.
- Steam Railway and Isle of Wight Line journeys.

Keeping the kids amused

- Robin Hill Country Park – Island Brass Rubbing Centre at Arreton – Amazon World.
- Blackgang Chine Theme Park – Dinosaur Farm Museum.
- Little Canada Adventure Park – drop the kids off and enjoy a day on your own.
- The Brading Experience – Amusement arcades at Sandown or Shanklin – IOW Zoo at Sandown – Dinosaur Isle.
- Shanklin Chine and the Undercliff.
- Needles Pleasure Park – Alum Bay.
- Godshill Model Village – Carisbrooke Castle.
- Isle of Wight Steam Railway and Museum at Havenstreet – Brickfields Horsecountry.

*Aerial view of
Yarmouth Castle*

COAST & COUNTRY
SCENIC DRIVES

- *About 30 miles:* Newport – Carisbrooke Castle – Chillerton (Gatcombe Church) – Chale Green – Chale – Blackgang – Niton – St Lawrence – Ventnor – Godshill – Newport.

- *About 35 miles:* Newport – West Cowes – Porchfield – Newtown – Shalfleet – Yarmouth – Wellow – Calbourne – Brighstone – Shorwell – Carisbrooke – Newport.

- *About 35 miles:* Yarmouth – Colwell – Alum Bay and the Needles – Freshwater Bay – Military Road – Chale – Chale Green – Shorwell – Brighstone – Mottistone – Hulverstone – Yarmouth.

- *About 35 miles:* Ryde – Seaview – St Helen's – Bembridge – Yaverland – Sandown – Brading – Ashey Down – Mersley Down – Havenstreet – Whippingham – East Cowes – Ryde.

- *The Big One (around the Island), about 75 miles:* Newport – Arreton Down – Mersley Down – Ashey Down – Yarbridge – Sandown – Shanklin – Bonchurch – Ventnor – St Lawrence – Niton – Blackgang – Chale – Military Road – Freshwater Bay – Alum Bay and the Needles – Yarmouth – Shalfleet – Newport.

WET WEATHER OPTIONS

Wet weather can spoil anyone's holiday, but, with preparation and a decent programme of undercover options, the Island still has a great deal to offer. Throughout the text attractions suitable in all weathers are indicated.

Fact File

HOW TO GET THERE

The island is linked to the mainland ports of Portsmouth, Lymington and Southampton (all in Hampshire) by car ferries and high-speed passenger services.

There are three major operators:

Hovertravel ☎ (01983) 811000, www.hovertravel.co.uk

Red Funnel ☎ (0870) 4448898, www.redfunnel.co.uk

Wightlink ☎ (0870) 582 7744, www.wightlink.co.uk

Car Ferry Services

Wightlink
Portsmouth to Fishbourne. 24 hour service. Journey time 45 minutes.

Lymington to Yarmouth. Journey time 30 minutes.

Red Funnel
Southampton to East Cowes. Journey time 60 minutes.

Foot Passenger Services

Foot Passengers can travel on any of the above car ferries plus:

Hovertravel
Portsmouth to Ryde. High speed passenger Hovercraft.
Journey time 9 minutes.

Connecting bus service with nominal charge between Portsmouth and Southsea Rail station and the Hovercraft terminal at Clarence Pier, Southsea. The bus meets all hovercraft arrivals and departs from the railway station on the hour and half hour depending upon the hovercraft timetable.

Wightlink
Portsmouth to Ryde. High speed passenger Catamaran.
Journey time 15 minutes.

Red Funnel
Southampton to West Cowes. High speed passenger ferry.
Journey time 22 minutes.

ACCOMMODATION

The range of accommodation on the island is extensive, with something to suit all tastes and pockets: the most basic camping sites exist with exclusive adults-only (in the best possible taste!) holiday centres, homely B&Bs with prestigious hotels.

Every year, Isle of Wight Tourism's comprehensive guide lists a daunting array of establishments. However, only those establishments which have contributed to the advertising costs are included. The two main ferry companies (Red Funnel and Wightlink) produce all inclusive holiday packages covering the full range of accommodation available on the Island. Tourist Informa-

tion Centres on the Island, all listed later in the Fact File, will also be pleased to provide up to date information.

Personal Favourites are listed below:

Catered accommodation

Expensive

New Holmwood Hotel, Cowes ☎ (01983) 292508

The Priory Bay Hotel, St Helens 2AA Rosettes ☎ (01983) 613146 www.priorybay.co.uk. Has private beach and sports facilities including 9-hole golf course.

The Royal Hotel, Ventnor, 2AA Rosettes ☎ (01983) 852186 www.royalhoteliow.co.uk

The Seaview Hotel, Seaview. 1AA Rosette ☎ (01983) 612711 www.seaviewhotel.co.uk

Middle range

Newnham Farm, Binstead ETC Gold Award ☎ (01983) 882423 www.newnhamfarm.co.uk

Rylstone Manor, Shanklin ETC Silver Award ☎ (01983) 862806

Burlington Hotel, Ventnor ETC Silver Award ☎ (01983) 852113

Inexpensive

Little Gatcombe Farm, Gatcombe ☎ (01983) 721580

North Court B&B, Shorwell ☎ (01983) 740415

Self Catering

Chilton Farm Cottages, Brighstone ☎ (01983) 740338 www.chiltonfarm.co.uk

Appuldurcombe Farm, Wroxall ☎ (01983) 840188 www.appuldurcombe.co.uk

Alternatively there are several rental agencies on the island that can be contacted directly:

Home from Home Holidays, Ventnor ☎ (01983) 854340

Bembridge Holiday Homes ☎ (01983) 873163

Holiday parks/centres/villages

Holiday parks/centres/villages provide a wide range of accommodation either in mobile homes, bungalows, lodges, chalets or apartments. This type of holiday is ideal for those who want the maximum facilities close to their accommodation. Prices for accommodation vary but this choice of holiday is ideal for larger families and where saving money is essential. The centres range from small family run enterprises to large national companies. Standards and facilities can vary greatly from park to park and it is always best to check which facilities are available during the shoulder months (April, May, June & Sept).

Fact File

Camping and Caravanning

There are plenty of camping and touring sites for caravanners and campers. Set in a variety of locations, both coastal and countryside, some offer a good range of facilities whilst others offer peace and quiet.

Youth Hostels

There are two hostels on the Island, at **Totland Bay** and **Sandown**.

CAR HIRE – SELF DRIVE

South Wight Rentals, Shanklin	☎ (01983) 864263
U Drive Car & Jeep Hire, Sandown	☎ (0800) 0926545
Esplanade Ryde	☎ (01983) 562322
Solent Self Drive, Cowes	☎ (01983) 282050

CYCLE HIRE

Wight Cycle Hire, Chessell Pottery	☎ (01983) 731888
	www.wightcyclehire.co.uk
Isle Cycle Hire, Yarmouth	☎ (01983) 760738
Battersby Cycles, 2 Hill Street, Ryde	☎ (01983) 562039

ENTERTAINMENT

Isle of Wight Night Clubs

Away from the hotels, the clubbing scene is centred on the larger holiday towns. Most operate a dress code which excludes trainers and on some nights denims. Smart casual is always safe. Southern Vectis runs a bus on Fridays and Saturdays for night-clubbers at £3.00 per person to a variety of destinations.

NEWPORT – **Temptation** is open Thursday, Friday and Saturday.

RYDE – **The Balcony**, which thinks itself 'the Place To Be' is on the Seafront, above the LA Bowl.

SANDOWN – The best-known and self-proclaimed 'Island Number 1 Night-club' is **Colonel Bogey's** at Fort Street, www.bogeys.co.uk.

Cinemas

Cineworld Multiplex Cinema, Coppins Bridge, Newport	☎ (0871) 2208000
The Commodore, Star Street, Ryde	☎ (0845) 1662397
Medina Movie Theatre, Medina Leisure Centre, Fairlee Road, Newport	☎ (01983) 527020

Above: Newchurch
Below: Cycling

Fact File

Theatres

Apollo Theatre,
Pyle Street, Newport   ☎ (01983) 527267

Medina Theatre,
Mountbatten Centre,
Fairlee Road, Newport   ☎ (01983) 527020

Ryde Theatre, Lind Street   ☎ (01983) 568099

Shanklin Theatre,
Steephill Road   ☎ (01983) 868000

Radio Stations

Isle of Wight Radio 1072FM & 107FM

EVENTS

Isle of Wight Tourism produces an annual list of the main events on the Island. Changes may occur and it is always best to check in advance with the main events hotline on ☎ (01983) 813818 or visit the website www.islandbreaks.co.uk. Some of the main events are:

MAY
Isle of Wight Walking Festival – from family fun walks to serious walking challenges in aid of local charities

Cycling Festival – May to September

JUNE
Yarmouth Maritime Festival incorporating the 'old gaffers'

Round the Island Yacht Race

Isle of Wight Garden Show at Osbourne House (month can vary)

Isle of Wight Music Festival

JULY
Royal Isle of Wight County Show

AUGUST
Cowes Week (1st week of August).

Two day Garlic Festival at Newchurch

Island Steam Show at Havenstreet

Cowes Classic Powerboat race (or September)

SEPTEMBER
Cycling Festival (month can vary)

MAPS

Ordnance Survey Outdoor Leisure 29, *Isle of Wight*, 2.5 inches: 1 mile/4cm:1km.

Ordnance Survey Landranger 196, *Solent and the Isle of Wight*, 1.25 inches:1 mile/2cm:1km.

Isle of Wight Official Tourist Map includes street plans and attractions.

Leaflets, maps and books are available from:

Isle of Wight Tourism, Mail Order Department, Westridge Centre, Brading Road, Ryde, Isle of Wight PO33 1QS ☎ (01983) 813818, Fax (01983) 823033 or from Isle of Wight Tourist Information Centres.

PUBS

The Island has a rich variety of hostelries, all different in character and atmosphere. Pubs, like their clients, go through phases and so the pubs selected below are those which are personal favourites.

Arreton
The Hare and Hounds. At the top of Arreton Downs, next to the Robin Hill Country Park, one of the oldest island pubs. Extensive menu with changing daily specials. Children welcome ☎ (01983) 523446.

Brading
The Bugle Inn. Traditional inn serving home-cooked dishes. Families welcome ☎ (01983) 407359.

Chale
The Wight Mouse Inn. Extremely popular family pub serving an excellent range of food, caters particularly well for children. Superb views towards The Needles and Tennyson Down ☎ (01983) 730431.

Freshwater
The Red Lion. Next to All Saints church. A comfortable pub, good range of food both lunchtime and evening. Children under 10 allowed only in the garden ☎ (01983) 754925.

Havenstreet
The White Hart. Busy former coaching inn with convivial atmosphere. Traditional food served, home-made pies a speciality. No family room but families can use the garden. Children's menu ☎ (01983) 883485.

Niton
The Buddle Inn. An extremely popular, hospitable pub, en route to and from St Catherine's Point Lighthouse ☎ (01983) 730243.

Shalfleet
New Inn. Traditional village pub with small family area. Opposite the church. Excellent food served in the restaurant ☎ (01983) 531314.

Shanklin

The Village Inn. Old Village. Extensive menu from salad platters to steaks. Children welcome when eating with parents but must stay in children's area or in garden ☎ (01983) 862514.

Shorwell

The Crown Inn. A typical village local with a large garden and bar area. Diverse menu. Popular with walkers, motorists and visitors to the nearby church. Families welcome, children's play area ☎ (01983) 740293.

Ventnor

The Spyglass Inn. Ventnor Bay. Wonderful location overlooking the sea. Renowned for its local fish dishes, particularly crab sandwiches. Children are welcome ☎ (01983) 855338.

RESTAURANTS

The Island has a vast selection of places to eat and covers all price ranges from the expensive to the cheap and cheerful. Some restaurants and cafés are open all year round, others open seasonally but wherever you find yourself on the island you are never far away from a cream tea or a good wholesome meal. Most of the larger island hotels have excellent value restaurants open to non-residents and some of these have been included in the recommendations.

Personal Favourites

Cowes

Spinnaker's Restaurant. New Holmwood Hotel, Egypt Point. Table d'Hôte lunches and dinners, Sunday Carvery, extensive à la carte menu. Wonderful views across the Solent to Southampton Water. Medium range prices ☎ (01983) 292508.

Bembridge

Windmill Hotel Restaurant. Steyne Road, Bembridge. ☎ (01983) 875806.
The restaurant uses fresh local produce, including Bembridge crab and Island Lamb.

Freshwater Bay

Farringford Hotel. Former home of Alfred, Lord Tennyson. The hotel is open to non-residents for meals and morning coffee, afternoon teas or just a drink in the bar. Ideal for traditional Sunday lunch. Medium prices
☎ (01983) 752500.

Godshill

Old Smithy Coffee Shop. One of the best tearooms on the Island, open all year round. Delicious homemade cakes and lunchtime specials. The best clothes shop on the Island is next to the coffee shop. ☎ (01983) 840364.

Willow Tree Tea Gardens and Restaurant. Attractive gardens centred around a willow tree planted in 1914. Cream teas the speciality but a good spot for lunch. Seasonal opening ☎ (01983) 840633.

Seaview

SeaView Hotel Restaurant. Close to the sea and using Island produce, this well-known establishment comprises two restaurants and a bar. Exotic seafood is a speciality. Booking recommended. Expensive but worth it. ☎ (01983) 612711.

The Priory Bay Hotel, Brasserie & Restaurant. Modern European cuisine in great location overlooking the Solent. ☎ (01983) 613146.

Yarmouth

George Hotel Brasserie. Next to the castle. Food is imaginative and decorative, fine view of the garden and sea from the dining room. Meals can be served outside. Medium price range ☎ (01983) 760331.

Ventnor

The Royal Hotel. A large elegant restaurant serving excellent food. Medium price range. ☎ (01983) 852186.

Crab Inn, Shanklin

Fact File

Aerial Sports

Flying training courses and half-hour trial lessons are available at the Isle of Wight Airport (Sandown) in Piper Cub and Grumman aircraft or in a helicopter ☎ (01983) 402402.

Aircraft pleasure flights fly from Isle of Wight Airport ☎ (01983) 408374.

Hang-gliding and paragliding takes place on the downs. Butterfly Paragliding ☎ (01983) 731611 and High Adventure ☎ (01983) 752322 provide tuition.

Vectis Gliding Club offer flights and lessons from Bembridge ☎ (01983) 873368.

Angling

There are opportunities for coarse fishing at **Rookley Country Park** and three commercial lakes at **Nettlecombe Farm**, Whitwell ☎ (01983) 730783. Seafishing takes place from piers and beaches while boat trips offshore and to the banks and forts of the Solent for mixed fishing are popular and easy to arrange. Scotties Tackle shops [in Newport ☎ (01983) 522115 and Sandown ☎ (01983) 404555] are worth consulting on local conditions and facilities with a highly informative and detailed web-site, www.scotties-tackle.co.uk

Fitness Centres

Urban Metro Gym, Smallbrook Stadium, Nr Ryde
☎ (01983) 612000

Fitness Factory, 1a Portland Street, Newport ☎ (01983) 528149

The Exercise Studio, Station Approach, Perowne Way, Sandown (air conditioning, creche) ☎ (01983) 406000

Golf

Visitors are welcome at all Island golf courses, with varying time, membership and experience requirements. A telephone call will confirm details. Green fees vary from £15-25 per day, with the exception of Westridge, Ryde which is cheaper.

Golf courses
18-hole
Freshwater Bay Golf Club ☎ (01983) 752955

Shanklin & Sandown Golf Club ☎ (01983) 403217

12-hole
Ventnor Golf Club ☎ (01983) 853326

9-hole
Cowes Golf Club ☎ (01983) 292303

St George's Down Newport	☎ (01983) 525076
Osborne Golf Club	☎ (01983) 295421
Ryde Golf Club	☎ (01983) 614809

Westridge Golf Centre,
Brading Rd, Ryde   ☎ (01983) 613131
9-hole pay as you play, Floodlit Driving Range, large Golf Shop and Senior and Junior tuition.

Putting and Crazy Golf
Brown's Golf Course, Culver Parade, Sandown

Sandham Gardens, Sandown

Esplanade Gardens, Shanklin

Northwood Park, West Cowes

Appley Gardens, Ryde

Puckpool Park, Seaview

Ice skating

Ryde Ice Arena ☎ (01983) 615155 – recreational skating and skates for hire.

Leisure centres

The Medina Leisure Centre at Newport   ☎ (01983) 523767

The Heights Health and Leisure Base,
Broadway, Sandown   ☎ (01983) 405594

Racquet Sports

Tennis
Courts are available at:
Newport (**Seaclose Park** – 3 courts and a skate park),
East Cowes (the **Esplanade**),
West Cowes (**Northwood Park** – 6 courts),
Ryde (**Puckpool Park**),
Sandown (**Sandham Gardens** – 5 courts),
Ventnor (**Ventnor Park**).

The Medina Leisure Centre at Newport ☎ (01983) 523767) has indoor short tennis and badminton courts.

Squash
The Heights Health and Leisure Base, Broadway, Sandown IOW
☎ (01983) 405594.

Swimming Pools

The Heights Health and Leisure Base, Broadway, Sandown ☎ (01983) 405594 (main and learner pool, with a café and gymnasium).

Medina Leisure Centre, Fairlee Road Newport ☎ (01983) 523767 (25m pool, learner pool and slide).

Ryde Waterside Pool, The Esplanade, Ryde ☎ (01983) 563656 (moveable roof and an outdoor paddling pool).

West Wight Swimming Pool, Queens Road, Freshwater ☎ (01983) 752168 (also has a large sports hall, gym and multi-purpose room).

Ten-pin bowling

LA Bowl, Ryde Esplanade ☎ (01983) 617070) is a modern ten-pin bowling alley with electronic scoring. There is also a Magic Galleon play area. The pier at Sandown also has a bowling facility.

Water Sports

Sailing

The Island offers unrivalled facilities for both power and sailing craft, with numerous marinas and yacht clubs. Two suggestions for those not bringing their own craft are:

Yacht charter – Windward sailing ☎ (01983) 612800, www.windwardsailing.co.uk

Medina Valley Centre, an RYA recognised sailing centre for all ages ☎ (01983) 522195, www.medinavalleycentre.org.uk

Surfing

Compton Bay is the pre-eminent place for surfing. The book to have is *Sail and Surf the Isle of Wight* by Stan Connolly and Staci Rivers.

Windsurfing

Learners will find the shallow and safe Seagrove Bay at Seaview and Silver Beach at Bembridge suitable places to avoid early embarrassment. Otherwise, tuition is available through **Wight Water Adventure Sports** on the beach in Sandown Bay ☎ (01983) 404987 or Offshore Sports in Shanklin ☎ (01983) 866269. The more experienced will want to hone their skills at Ryde, Yaverland, Gurnard and Compton and avoid the crowds on the more popular beaches.

Wight Water also offers splash sessions – 3-hour sessions of water sports for families, together with tuition in canoeing and other water sports.

TAXIS

COWES:	**Anywhere Taxi**	☎ (01983) 281711
	Rounsevell Taxis	☎ (01983) 280800
NEWPORT:	**Amar Cabs**	☎ (01983) 522968
	Solo Cars	☎ (01983) 525010
	3Cs	☎ (01983) 825029
RYDE:	**Amber Cabs**	☎ (01983) 812222
	IOW Taxis	☎ (01983) 617027
	Lil's Taxis	☎ (01983) 562130
	Q Cars	☎ (01983) 810810
	Ryde Taxis	☎ (01983) 811111
SHANKLIN:	**A Cabs**	☎ (01983) 866772
YARMOUTH:	**Yarmouth Taxi Rank** ☎ (01983) 760024	

TOURIST INFORMATION CENTRES

Isle of Wight Tourism Central Office   ☎ (01983) 813818
Open daily throughout the year but closed on some days in
January and February. Ventnor TIC seasonal, March-October.

Cowes, The Arcade Fountain Quay	☎ (01983) 291914
Newport, The Guildhall	☎ (01983) 823366
Ryde, The Esplanade	☎ (01983) 562905
Sandown, The Esplanade	☎ (01983) 403886
Shanklin, High Street	☎ (01983) 862942
Ventnor, High St	☎ (01983) 853625
Yarmouth, The Quay	☎ (01983) 760015

WEB SITES

www.islandbreaks.co.uk – the Isle of Wight Tourism official web
site.

www.isle-of-wight.uk.com – a compendium of advertisers, associations and links to hundreds of Island web sites.

www.netguides.co.uk/wight – miscellaneous outline information
about the Island.

www.wightonline.co.uk – another general information site.

www.english-heritage.org.uk

www.nationaltrust.org.uk

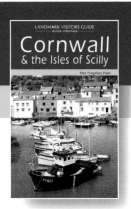

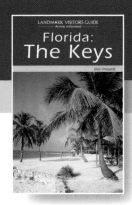

UK   *World*   *Europe*

Northern Cyprus (2nd Edition)	1-84306-158-9	£10.95
New Forest (3rd Edition)	1-84306-214-3	£6.50
North Devon & Exmoor (1st Edition)	1-84306-142-2	£7.95
North Wales & Snowdonia	1-84306-043-4	£9.95
Oxford	1-84306-022-1	£3.95
Peak District (2nd Edition)	1-84306-097-3	£9.95
Puerto Rico	1-901522-34-2	£7.95
Riga & its beaches, Latvia (2nd Edition)	1-84306-096-5	£9.95
Rhodes	1-84306-121-X	£10.95
Shakespeare Country & the Cotswolds (2nd Ed)		
	1-84306-101-5	£10.95
Somerset (2nd Edition)	1-84306-117-1	£10.99
St Lucia (5th Edition)	1-84306-178-3	£6.99
Zakinthos (2nd Edition)	1-84306-024-8	£7.50

Prices subject to change

Landmark Publishing Ltd
Ashbourne Hall, Cokayne Ave, Ashbourne, Derbyshire, DE6 1EJ England
Tel 01335 347349   Fax 01335 347303   e-mail landmark@clara.net

Published in the UK by
Landmark Publishing Ltd,
Ashbourne Hall, Cokayne Ave, Ashbourne, Derbyshire DE6 1EJ England
Tel: (01335) 347349 Fax: (01335) 347303 e-mail: sales@landmarkpublishing.co.uk
website: www.landmarkpublishing.co.uk

4th Edition, 2006
ISBN: 1-84306-217-8

Print: Gutenberg Press Ltd, Malta
Design: James Allsopp

Front cover: Horse-drawn carriage rides at Osborne House
Back cover, top: Shanklin Old Village
Back cover, bottom: The Needles

Picture Credits:

Isle of Wight Tourism – www.islandbreaks.co.uk:
Back cover T, Back cover B, p7, p8, p10, p12B, p13T, p13B, p17T, p17M, p17B, p19, p30, p32, p35, p37, p38, p40, p46, p47, p49, p54/55, p61, p66, p67, p68, p70, p69, p82, p84/85, p88, p89 & p99B

Classic Boat Museum, Newport: p57

English Heritage: p45, p61, p56 & p94

Patrick Eden: p26/27, p29 & p67

Peter Titmuss: p12T, p20, p51, p60, p75, p76, p87, p93 & p99T

International Photobank: Cover, p3, p23 & p24

Southern Tourist Board: p31, p48, p59 & p103

3D Education and Adventure Ltd: p53